# DO YOU SPEAK ASTROLOGY?

### Learn The Language of the Skies

### To Help Understand Yourself, Your Career,

### Your Relationships

## BY
# DOE  DONOVAN

D1599428

Library of Congress Catalog Card Number  91-066798


ISBN 0-945-27-05-2

Published by
Sparrow Hawk Press,
22 Summit Ridge Dr.
Tahlequah, OK 74464
(918) 456-3421

# ACKNOWLEDGMENTS

My husband, Len Koppana, for continued encouragement, help and love.

My family, friends, teachers and students from whom I have learned so much. My children, whom I know so well and saw reflected in their Natal Charts, especially my sons, Jay, Sean and Paul Hogan who took pride in my work, with special thanks to Sean for giving me an extra push. Great appreciation of the outstanding suggestions from Donna Lafferty after she read the manuscript, and input from her husband Tim. Thanks to Adele and Tom Lippert, and their sons, Paul and Mark for special suggestions, and thanks to Bettye Erikson, and her daughter Margaret Trousdale, for their input. Proof reading thanks to my sister Marge Donovan Young, Tom Lippert and my husband. Thanks to my sister Trish Donovan who kept me up with news from the "outside world" when I became immersed in my work. Appreciation of technical dedication from Gloria Riehl and technical input from my brother-in-law Jim Young. Thanks to Charles Harra, publisher of Sparrow Hawk Press, and his staff, for gracious cooperation on this project.

And finally in memory of my mother and father who created a home that encouraged learning and communicating, and gave me loving sisters and brothers who have been a life long joy.

# TABLE OF CONTENTS

# FOREWORD

Have you ever wondered why the Earth has the right number of people who want to be teachers, or doctors, clerks, carpenters, hair stylists, pilots, actors, cooks, street cleaners, accountants, journalists, artists, etc.? Is it just a coincidence that everyone wouldn't want the same glamorous, high-paying job? Astrology shows the temperament of the individual. It can show the career inclinations in people born at different times of the day and year. It is a complex, but fascinating subject. It is like a magic key for understanding yourself and other people.

Many prominent people have managers, or agents, or public relations experts to give them guidance in making the best decisions in their careers. Those of us who don't have managers can use the objective understanding of our Natal Charts to help us see our options and opportunities in life. That way we can better "manage" our lives and make the best choices.

Astrology, like music, can be enjoyed at all levels - - from the playing of a simple melody all the way to scoring a major work for a symphony orchestra. How proficient you want to become is your decision. The fastest way to make astrology part of you is to immerse yourself in it as if you were using the Berlitz Method of foreign language study. The easiest way to do this is with your own Natal Chart as a constant reference point.

Astrology should be taught as a conversational language. It is a universal language. The most exciting and immediate way to use a language is on a conversational level. This is my approach to teaching astrology. This book can be used just to understand astrology, or it can be used to help you "speak the language of the skies."

In addition to the Constellations and Planets, which are always capitalized, all astrological terms will be capitalized as a visual aid in learning.

# HOW TO USE THIS BOOK

If you wish only to get a general understanding of astrology, read the following sections: Basic Astrology; The Planets; The Sun Signs; and the Aspects. For information on career potential and personal relationships, read Career Indicators and Relationships (after the major chapters just listed). The section on Interpretation shows how all the pieces fit in individual Charts. Rectification explains how Charts are figured out when the exact time of birth is not known. The Reference Section is to be used once you have a computerized list of your Chart.

If you want to be really fluent in astrology, you have to memorize the basics, just as you would learn basic phrases in another language. You must "drill yourself" on the four foundations of astrology. Read and reread the important parts of this book whenever you can. Write key information in note form to carry with you. When you're alone in a restaurant, or in a waiting room, study the notes. For ten minutes every night - just before you go to sleep - read parts of it. Read more astrology books from your library. As a teacher, I always used visual aids, so the book is full of them. I also like word associations, so I've included all the ones I've developed in teaching astrology.

As you continue studying, you should get a copy of your Natal Chart. There are several good Astrological Computer Services. The cost is usually about $5.00 for the Natal Chart. A Computerized interpretative Chart costs about $20.00 to $25.00. If there is no astrology/service in your city, you can obtain a Natal Chart and/or interpretive Chart from Astro Computing Services, P.O. Box 16430, San Diego, CA 92116. )There are courses taught on the mathematical/astronomical calculations used in constructing a Chart for those interested). An astrological Natal Chart done by a computer is only part of the interpretation that can be done. It does not usually contain an analysis of the Planets in the various Signs of the Zodiac. More importantly, it is not capable of pulling the Chart together as a whole. Nor does it explain conflicting energies from Aspects involving the same Planets. But it will give you a great deal of information about yourself, and can be a wonderful personal introduction to astrology. Later, you might find it interesting and extremely helpful to have your Chart done by a competent astrologer. The results should give you a psychological profile of the most important person in your life - yourself.

1

*Introduction
to Basic
Astrology*

Some years ago, a friend of mine asked me if I believed in Astrology. I answered, "I don't believe it, or disbelieve it. I don't know anything about it, so I can't make a valid judgement." She said that she had a friend who was an astrologer, and if I would give her my exact time of birth, she would have her friend do a brief analysis of my Chart. A month later my friend read the notes to me, and as Johnny Carson would say, she knocked my socks off! This triggered my interest in astrology. I began studying astrology as if I were an investigative reporter. I wanted to explore its validity.

The first thing that I learned about astrology was that your Sun Sign is the most important part of your Natal Chart. But there are two other factors that are also tremendously important -- the Ascendant and the Moon. The Ascendant is the Degree and Sign that is on the eastern horizon at the moment of your birth. It describes your outward personality.

To help you understand how the Ascendant works in combination with the Sun Sign, I'll tell you about an incident that happened a few years ago. I was teaching a series of astrology classes at a private club in Cincinnati. As I walked through the dining room, I saw the world-class baseball player and Hall of Fame member, Johnny Bench, having lunch with two friends. He and I share the same birthday, which was only two days away. My Sun Sign is Sagittarius, the most outgoing of all the Signs. The inner part of me, represented by the Sun, wanted to go over to Johnny Bench and wish him a happy birthday and tell him that we shared the same birthday. I wanted to tell him also that I had recently been explaining to my astrology class how different people could be who were born on the same day but in two different years. My Ascendant is Pisces, one of the two shyest Signs. I had been a very shy child with strangers. My Sun was urging me to go out and say hello, while my Ascendant personality was telling me that I couldn't do that because I didn't know him. After being pulled in two directions, my Sun finally won out. When I introduced myself to Johnny Bench, wished him a happy birthday and told him about my class, he surprised me by telling me what his Ascendant and Moon Signs are, as well as other prominent Planets in his Chart. He said that an astrologer from California had written to him asking for his birth information, and then had sent him a written analysis of his birth Chart. He said he was amazed by the information.

So your Sun Sign and Ascendant are very strong, but different parts of you. Astrology helps you understand the differences to integrate them more fully. The Moon Sign will describe your emotional nature and your sub-conscious mind. The Moon changes Signs approximately every 2 to 2 1/2 days. The Ascending Sign changes about every 2 hours, going through all twelve Constellation Signs in one 24-hour period. So someone born on the same day as you could have any one of twelve different personality types (depending on which Sign was ascending), and if the Moon changed Signs on that day, there would be a different emotional nature. The possible number of combinations of the Sun and Ascendant Signs is 144; when you add the 12 possible Moon Signs to this, the number jumps to 1,728 possible combinations. And this is only part of the Chart!

When I first introduce my students to the Sun, Moon and

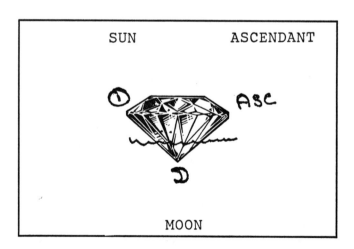

Ascendant, I draw a diamond from a side view. I explain that our impression of someone is a combination of their Sun and Ascendant. Are they a diamond chip, 1/2 karat, 1 karat, 3 karats, or a "Liz Taylor rock?" Is the person a brilliant cut, an emerald cut, a marquise cut, a pear shape? So we get a sense of the person from these two points. The Moon in astrology, representing our emotional nature and the sub-conscious mind, is beneath the surface. So I show it beneath the setting of the ring in the diagram. But all light and color in the diamond is refracted through this bottom point, just as all thoughts are filtered through our sub-conscious mind and colored by our emotions.

Astrology is empirical knowledge. That is knowledge through observation and experience. It is scientific in its astronomical calcualtions. It is an ancient art in its interpretation, which continues to grow. Astrology is based on complete free will.

## HOW TO VISUALIZE YOUR SUN SIGN

The Earth is like a spinning top as it orbits around the Sun. Our view from Earth shows a slowly changing backdrop of the stars in the twelve Constellations during a year. When we use the words "Sun Sign," we are referring to the starry background that we see behind the Sun. The stars that make up the Conctellations are called fixed stars (although they are moving imperceptively farther out) in contrast to Planets which revolve around the Sun.

If you invision sitting in a theatre with a curved stage backdrop of the Constellations, you would see a different angle of the backdrop from different sections of the theatre.

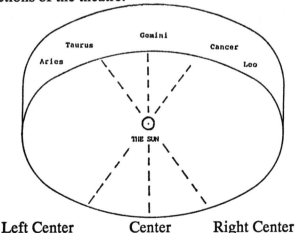

Left     Left Center     Center     Right Center     Right

If you were seated in the center section, the center-line backdrop would be Gemini. If you were seated in right center, the backdrop would be Taurus. If you were seated in left center, the backdrop would be Cancer. So, as the Earth follows its ecliptic path around the Sun, the Sun appears to have a different Constellation background from our view on Earth. On the day you were born, the Sun's "backdrop Constellation" is your Sun Sign.

## EVERYDAY EVIDENCE OF THE INFLUENCE OF THE SUN AND MOON

Some effects of the Sun and Moon are known to us. The Sun has "Sun Spots" which create static interference in radio and television broadcasts. The Sun Spots charge the electro-magnetic fields of the Earth which cause the aurora borealis, or northern lights. Many people are aware of the gravitational pull of the Moon. The effects that we know of from the cycles of the Moon are planting on the new Moon and harvesting on the full Moon, except for root crops, which are planted on the waning Moon. So, if you want something to be successful in the public eye, you plant it, or start it, on the new Moon. I think that is why many businesses open on a new Moon. The Moon's gravitational pull helps the body retain fluids during the full Moon. More babies are born during a full Moon. There are more crimes committed, there are more angina attacks, there is more activity in mental institutions (which used to be called lunatic asylums from the Latin word, luna, which means Moon). There is more hemorrhaging during surgery, and there are more fires started by arsonists.

An Associated Press article, appearing in the Cincinnati Enquirer on January 8, 1982, quoted Professor Ralph Morris of the University of Chicago's Medical Center linking the effects of illness to the full Moon. It was a pharmacology study showing the relationship of medication as being extremely important during full Moon phases. The Journal of American Medical Association published his findings in its January 8, 1982 issue. Morris studied more than 100 patients over five years and found that bleeding ulcers and chest pains became more frequent in two-thirds of the patients at times of a full Moon.

Allen Hynek, Professor emeritus of Physics and Astronomy at Northwestern University, was quoted in the same article concerning the effects of lunar cycles on humans saying that some people "just pooh-poohed this as astrology. I don't think it should be." Hynek cited studies showing increases in arson, violent crimes and strange behavior in mental hospitals when the Moon is full.

Some astrologers say that they don't know how astrology works, but only that it does work. It has always seemed to me to be one of Aristotle's five proofs for the existence of God — the order of the universe. Since we understand the tremendous effects of the Sun (it's necessary for all life on Earth) and the Moon, I think it is the gravitational pull of all the Planets which cause the Planetary influences described in a Chart. Some effects of other Planets will be discussed in later chapters. I think of the Planets as a "giant computer in the sky," programming certain temperaments, personalities, talents, career inclinations, etc., so that there will be the right number of people to fill the huge variety of necessary jobs in this world. Psychologists say that we are born with our individual temperament. How we go from there is up to us. Learning about ourselves through astrology gives us wonderful help in making good decisions and choices.

## WHAT ASTROLOGY CAN DO FOR YOU

There are frequent articles in the newspapers about scientists finding validity in astrology. You will find some of them quoted in this book. Before I became a professional astrologer, and started clipping these articles, there were several interesting ones in our local morning paper. One of them was by a reporter who wanted to investigate astrology. He had his Chart done by a local astrologer, which cost $50.00. He then took a battery of tests from a group of PhD's to obtain a psychological profile. This cost $500.00. He said that the information he received from both sources was essentially the same.

So, having your Chart done can give you tremendous insight. The continued study of my own Chart has given me the confidence to go in a new career direction full force. When I first had my Chart done, it was at a major turning point in my design career. Understanding my true potential, I stopped hovering on the edge of the nest, working with an interior design company, and started my own design business. My career took off.

My eldest son thinks that astrology is like a road map showing you many different routes that you can choose, and indicating the most favorable direct route. He also feels that astrology took what he believed about God, creation, life and death from the realm of faith and put it into everyday perspective.

## HISTORICAL BACKGROUND

There are many fine books on the historical development of astrology for an in-depth study. To touch briefly on the historical part, astrology was the forerunner of astronomy. All astronomers were astrologers until the Scientific Revolution in the 17th Century. The observation of the stars and Planets dates back many thousand of years in history. There are astrological artifacts dating from the 7th century B.C., and astrological records from 5,000 years ago.

Sailors and shepherds studied the stars in ancient times. The sailors used stars for navigation. Many people began to notice certain configurations of the stars during different seasons of the year. They imagined that some of the groupings looked like animals such as the Ram, the Bull, the Lion, etc. If you studied the Constellations to try to see the animals, you would have to try to picture the stars in a sort of ``connect-a-dot'' pattern. There is a twin column of stars in the Constellation of Gemini - thus, the symbol for Gemini became the Twins.

The Chaldeans and the Babylonians contributed much toward the development of accurate observations of the Planets and Constellations. The Chaldeans were excellent mathematicians. They were the first to observe the regular patterns of Planetary movement. They developed the first written ephemerides (records showing Planetary position by longitude at different times of the year) during the mid-7th century B.C.

Planets represented gods to ancient people. In Babylonia, the Planet Mercury was thought of as the god of wisdom and cunning. Mars was the god of war and violence. Jupiter was a fair, beneficent ruler.

Saturn was seen as a harsh and cruel god. The god-like Planets developed into the astrological beliefs of Planetary influence.

The Egyptians, Greeks and Romans made great use of astrology. There are many historical artifacts from these civilizations which can be seen today. The illustrations of the Zodiac Signs which are used in this book are from the bas relief on the ceiling of the Temple of the Ram Headed God Khnum near Luxor, Egypt. The temple is over 2,000 years old.

The magnificent pyramids of Egypt were built as tombs and as astrological observatories more than four thousand years ago. Observations of very accurate astrological calculations could be achieved.

The Greeks developed the names for the Zodiac which the Romans converted to Latin. The names used today are from the Latin. The term Zodiac is from the Greek, meaning "ring of animals."

One of the most interesting remains of ancient astrological observatories is the monument at Stonehenge in England. Dating back to 2500 B.C., Stonehenge was used as an excellent visual calendar. The solstices and eclipses could be predicted through it.

Astrology was not practiced in Europe during the Dark Ages. At this time astrology was used and further developed by Islamic Arabia. There are many "Arabian parts" still used in astrology today.

Astrology flourished during Renaissance times. There were Astrological chairs in the major universities in Europe. Most of the royal courts had court astrologers. Pope Julius II, who commissionsed many of Michelangelo's magnificent works, had a court astrologer. Pope Pius X was a gifted amateur astrologer. The Christmas Liturgy used in the Catholic Church is now translated to read "the three astrologers" instead of "the three wise men." In ancient times, astrologers were called the wise men.

Until, 1601, it was believed that the Sun revolved around the Earth. Astrologer, astronomer, mathematician Johannes Kepler, of Prague, proved that the Earth revolved around the Sun. In retrospect, what should have expanded the knowledge of astrology actually signaled the beginning of its decline in popularity. The astrology of the 17th century worked, but suddenly the basis for this system was astronomically different from what had been assumed for thousands of years. It was a case of a new and wonderful scientific discovery not being properly assimilated with the ancient theories of astrology. But Kepler wrote before he died that no one who had studied astrology could doubt its validity.

The Scientific Revolution of the 17th century caused a separation of astronomy from astrology, with astrology falling into disfavor. The decline of astrology was further influenced by charlatans who misused astrology during this period. There has been a rebirth of interest in astrology during the approach to the age of Aquarius.

Some people question the compatibility of religion and astrology. Thomas Aquinas, the great 13th century philosopher and theologian, reconciled the Christian doctrine of free will with astrology. The doctrines written by Aquinas are the foundation of Catholic philosophy which is taught in most Catholic colleges and universities. He expresses his acceptance of astrology in his famous Summa Theologica. His theory of free will and astrological influence is similar to that of modern astrology.

Bible scholar, astrologer Don Jacobs has written a book entitled Astrology's Pew In Church, which is worthwhile reading for anyone concerned about religion with astrology. There is an outstanding reference book available in paperback which covers the history of astrology, as well as the complete subject of astrology. It is the Larousse Encyclopedia of Astrology by Jean-Louis Brau, Helen Weaver and Allan Edmunds. A visually rich, and thoroughly detailed book is The Compleat Astrologer by Derek and Julia Parker.

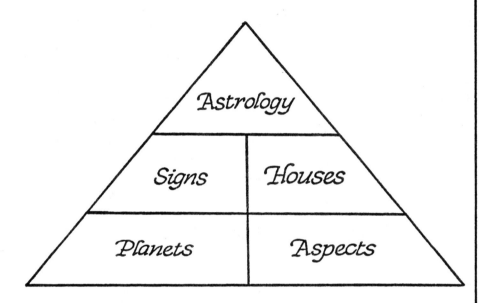

*Astrology is pyramid learning*

*The four foundation stones of astrology*

# THE SUN SIGNS
## (The First Foundation Stone)

| ZODIAC SIGN | GLYPH | SYMBOL | MEMORY ASSOCIATION |
|---|---|---|---|
| 1. Aries | ♈ | The Ram | The Ram's Horn (can butt ahead) |
| 2. Taurus | ♉ | The Bull | The Bull's Head (can be bull headed) |
| 3. Gemini | ♊ | The Twins | Twin columns of stars as seen in the Gemini Constellation<br>Likes to do two things at the same time |
| 4. Cancer | ♋ | The Crab | The nurturing Sign, showing the cradling of a loved one<br>The crab carrying its home on its back |
| 5. Leo | ♌ | The Lion | The tail of the lion, the king of the jungle. Leo is the Sign of nobility |
| 6. Virgo | ♍ | The Virgin | The Letter M with its leg tucked modestly. Virgos like to work unnoticed |
| 7. Libra | ♎ | The Scales | Looks like a balancing scale<br>The symbol of justice. Libras are fair judges |
| 8. Scorpio | ♏ | The Scorpion | The letter M with a stinger attached for self-protection |
| 9. Sagittarius | ♐ | The Centaur/ Archer | The arrow of the hunter searching for the truth |
| 10. Capricorn | ♑ | Mountain Goat | A ram's horn with the letter S, or a tail showing the circuitous climb up the mountain |
| 11. Aquarius | ♒ | Water Bearer | Looks like ocean waves (Can also be drawn with sharp lines -- as it represents electric current). |
| 12. Pisces | ♓ | The Fish | Two fish tied together, swimming in opposite directions |

| PLANET | GLYPH | MEANING | MEMORY ASSOCIATION |
|---|---|---|---|
| Sun | ☉ | The will, basic core, character | The circle of the Sun |
| Moon | ☽ | Emotional nature, sub-conscious mind | The crescent-shaped moon |
| Mercury | ☿ | Communications, mentality | A circle and a cross, with antennae for broadcasting |
| Venus | ♀ | Beauty, harmony ability to love | A hand mirror |
| Mars | ♂ | Physical energy, ego energy | The shield of protection, The arrow of aggression |
| Jupiter | ♃ | Expansion, growth, good fortune | A number 2 that expands to a number 4 |
| Saturn | ♄ | Responsibilities, boundaries, structure, limitation | The letter h, with a hat on it, to hold things in and cap them down |
| Uranus | ♅ | Sudden change, ingenuity, rebellion | A goal post with a wrecking ball to force change |
| Neptune | ♆ | Idealism, imagination, spirituality, disillusion | The trident of King Neptune of the sea |
| Pluto | ♇ | Regeneration, unforced change, power | The combination of the letters P and L. Also looks like a steam shovel |

## The Houses
### (The Third Foundation Stone)

House systems were developed to show three dimensional space in a flat, two dimensional form. There are several different house systems being used by astrologers today. The Charts in this book are all based on the Placidian House System. The Placidus System was developed by Placidus de Tito, a 17th century monk. This is the most popular system used by American astrologers. Another system which has been gaining popularity during the past decade is the Koch System, developed by German astrologer, Dr. Walter Koch. There are two types of Natal Charts: geocentric (geo meaning Earth and centric meaning the center), and heliocentric (helio meaning Sun). The Charts used in this book are geocentric, so the view of the Planets has the Earth in the middle of the Chart, with the longitude and latitude of your birthplace in the exact center.

The Houses are a circle representing the 360 Degrees of the Zodiac. The circle is divided into twelve sections, or parts, which represent twelve different areas of life. The first six Houses represent the individual. The second six represent the individual in relation to the outer world.

Some of the Houses represent more categories than others. When you are learning the meanings of the Houses, study the visual memory associations from the illustrated wheel. When you need to, refer to the following descriptions of all the House activities.

FIRST HOUSE          The Self. How you look physically. How you project through personality.

SECOND HOUSE     Self-earned money. Your values. The ability and talent that you have to earn money.

THIRD HOUSE         Communication. Close contacts -- your brothers and sisters, your neighbors, your immediate environment, short trips. The mundane mind. Lower education.

FOURTH HOUSE — Your roots -- your parents and your home. The beginning and ending of life. Your security.

FIFTH HOUSE — Creativity -- the creations of your mind and body. Love affairs. The Sign on the Fifth House Cusp usually indicates the type of person (through their Sun, Moon, or Ascendant) that we are attracted to romantically. Fun and games.

SIXTH HOUSE — The House of work and service -- what you do to earn a living. Health -- the Sign on the Cusp relates to possible health problems.

SEVENTH HOUSE — The House of partnership -- business or marriage. Also can represent a very close personal friendship. Public relations. The lower courts.

EIGHTH HOUSE — The House of regeneration. Partner's money and other people's assets involved with you. Inheritances. Insurance. The in-depth House concerned with life, death and the unknown. Sexuality. The Sign on the Cusp describes your attitude toward sex.

NINTH HOUSE — The higher (abstract) mind and subjects related to it including philosophy, the law and the higher courts, religion, publishing, and higher education. Long distance travel.

TENTH HOUSE — Your public image -- professionally and/or socially. Reputation. The career you strive to achieve. There is a secondary meaning that the Sign on the Cusp represents your stronger parent (and therefore the Fourth House can represent your other parent). Social prestige and/or power.

ELEVENTH HOUSE The House of goals -- what you wish for and work toward in life. This also represents the money House of your career (in contrast to the Second which shows the ability you have to make money). The Sign on the Cusp shows the type of Sun Sign person you are attracted to as a friend.

TWELFTH HOUSE The behind-the-scenes House. Seclusion. Meditation, mental health. Institutions, including universities, physical and mental hospitals. The Sign on the Cusp can indicate the type of any possible hospitalization. The subconscious mind.

## A Visualization of The Houses

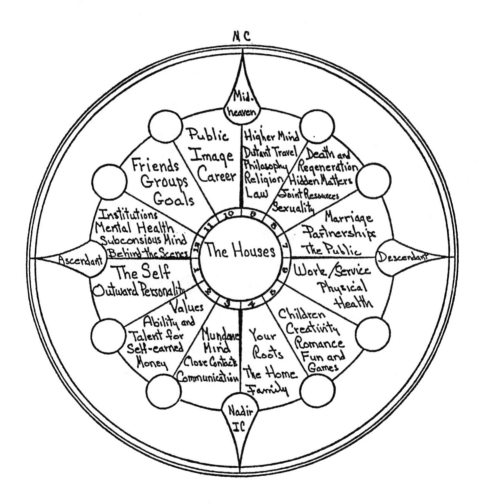

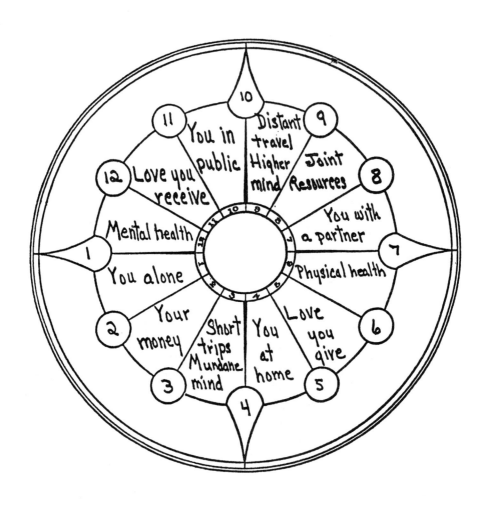

# THE HOUSE CONNECTIONS

The first six Houses are personal, involving you alone. The second six have a connecting link with the House at the opposite point.

# THE ASPECTS
## (The Fourth Foundation Stone)

The fourth foundation stone of astrology is what is called the Aspects. Aspects are important specific geometric angles formed between Planets. There are six significant Aspects. The first Aspect occurs when two Planets are in the same line of celestial longitude, within an orb of seven Degrees or less. The next Aspect is when two Planets are sixty Degrees apart. The remaining four Aspects are each an additional thirty Degrees further apart — at 90 Degrees, 120 Degrees, 150 Degrees and 180 Degrees. These Aspects, or contacts, between the Planets stimulate activity that will be harmonious or inharmonious depending on which Aspect is formed. When teaching astrology, I hold the Aspects aside until the other three foundation stones are securely in place.

# The Foundation Stones in Detail

## THE SUN SIGNS

The Sun Signs represent 12 different character types. The good qualities in our Sign are what we should strive to become. The temperament described by each Sign shows what we are capable of achieving. Astrological belief is firmly based on free will. So, the choice is ours. As you study your Sun Sign, concentrate on accentuating the fine qualities of the Sign and guarding against the problem areas.

Before reading the description of the Sun Signs, there are several factors to keep in mind:

1.      The Sun represents the potential temperament of the individual. This influence can have a positive or negative expression, depending on your free will.

2.      The Sun characteristics can be inhibited by several factors:

   a.      If the Planet Saturn is Conjunct (within 7 Degrees) the Sun Sign personality can be restricted, and sometimes the characteristics are almost invisible to others. But the inner person should have the basic qualities described in the Sign.

   b.      Very shy or quiet rising Signs make it difficult to see the Sun Sign characteristics.

   c.      The Sun can be in an intercepted Sign (interceptions are explained in the chapter on the Mechanics of the Chart).

   d.      If the Sun falls in the 12th House, the characteristics may be hidden from view, and therefore not prominent.

3.    The dates for the various Signs are approximate. These are the dates which are usually the changing dates, but the exact date can change by a day depending on the year. To determine your correct Sign if you were born close to the beginning or ending of a Sign (called the Cusp in astrology), you need to check an ephemeris for the day and year you were born. This is done astronomically when you order a computer Chart.

Also, the Sun does not change Signs at midnight, but can change at different times of the day. This is why the exact time of birth is so important.

4.    We start with Aries on what is referred to as a natural wheel. For thousands of years, the first day of spring (which is when the Sun moves to zero Degrees of Aries) was always the beginning of the new year. It wasn't until England adopted the Julian Calendar in the 1752 that the new year began on the first day of January in English-speaking countries.

The illustrations for the Sun Signs in this chapter are drawings of the bas relief on the ceiling of the Temple of the Ram headed god, Khnum. The Temple is located near Luxor, Egypt and was built more than 2,000 years ago.

ARIES

Approximate Dates:                     Quality:  Cardinal
March 21 - April 19                  Element:  Fire
Symbol:  The Ram                   Ruling Planet:  Mars

| HAS: | IS: | LIKES: | NEEDS: | THE MOST: |
|---|---|---|---|---|
| Courage | Assertive | Being First | Achieve- | Physically |
| Energy | Leader | Independence | ments | Active |
| Ambition | Impulsive | Pioneering | Action | |

# ARIES

Aries people are usually easy to spot. Their energy vibrations seem to jump right out of their skin. This is the Sign of the pioneer, the explorer — the people who dare to rush in where angels fear to tread. Courage and quick action are pronounced. Aries people are natural leaders. They have the skill and fearlessness to make it to the top in their chosen professions. Fame is more important to them than money. This is an aggressive competitive Sign. Aries can be impulsive with money. Because of their impulsive nature, they dislike a passive approach to problem solving.

This is the most physically active of all the Signs. Aries produces many fine athletes and dancers. This is also true when the Planet Mars falls in Aries. This is the Sign of the hero and/or leader. Like their symbol of the ram, Aries people will be headstrong, will butt right in and forge ahead.

They are uncomplicated people. They like to initiate many new projects, but sometimes they don't like to stick around to see the projects to their conclusions. This is the "me first" Sign, so Aries people can be self-centered. Aries is the natural ruler of the First House of astrology. This is the House of "the self."

Being so energetic, Aries people always seem to be "on the go." They have terrific drive and they love to win. Because their natural action is so quick, they can be impatient. They also need to develop the ability to really listen to others.

The late astrologer, Don Jacobs (Moby Dick), said that with Aries people you needn't say, "Don't just stand there, do something," but rather, "Don't just do something, stand there!"

**TAURUS**

Approximate Dates:
April 20 - May 20
Symbol: The Bull

Quality: Fixed
Element: Earth
Ruling Planet: Venus

| HAS: | IS: | LIKES: | NEEDS: | THE MOST: |
|---|---|---|---|---|
| Determination | Moneymaker | Security | Time to adjust | Determined |
| Patience | Attractive | Food | to new things | |
| Perseverance | Sensual | The Country- | Peace, serenity | |
| Ability to | Hard working | side | | |
| visualize form | | To sit | | |

# TAURUS

Taurus people are strong, slow moving and steady. They have a great love of beauty since the Sign is ruled by Venus. Taurus has a sense of beauty and form. Taurus is a very sensuous Sign. They make very sensuous lovers. There is great love of beautiful possessions and good food. Taurus is one of the three money-making Signs, which enables them to buy the things they love. They are usually very astute at business. Taurus is the natural ruler of the Second House of values and possessions. There is also great love of land, and therefore ownership of property. Tauruses get their strength from the Earth. You'd seldom find a Taurus living in a mobile home! They are the most fixed of the fixed Signs, and therefore the most stubborn. They are slow to assimilate and digest new ideas.

This is a peace loving Sign with a placid temperament. Taurus people are slow to anger, but when they do get angry, look out! It's as if a red flag were waved in front of a bull. Don't try to reason or argue with them when they are aroused. This is the Sign of the bull that can become a bully when angered. They can annihilate you if you get in the way.

If you're looking for someone who's generous, this is the Sign. Tauruses lavish their loved ones with gifts. Taurus husbands especially like to give their wives necklaces and pendants, since Taurus rules the throat.

There is a wonderful solid, reliable quality to the Taurus person. They usually have good powers of visualization. Many Taurus-born people can be found among artists who work as sculptors or wood workers. A large number work as builders, utilizing their ability to see form and combine it with their love of property and land. Because they are so deliberate, Tauruses can be slow in deciding their careers.

There is a strong love of nature among people with this Sign. They especially enjoy springtime with the blossoming trees and flowers. When you think of Taurus, picture Ferdinand the Bull sitting placidly in the meadow smelling the flowers. Taurus people like to sit so much that they can be lazy, once they sit. But don't ever forget the strength and power of the bull!

GEMINI

Approximate Dates:
May 21 - June 21
Symbol: The Twins

Quality: Mutable
Element: Air
Ruling Planet: Mercury

| HAS: | IS: | LIKES: | NEEDS: | THE MOST: |
|------|-----|--------|--------|-----------|
| Verbal Skills | Social | Collecting data | Two Major | Mentally |
| Nervous-energy | Versatile | Distributing data | Interests | Active |
| Awareness | Adaptable | Activity | Time to wind | |
| Love of learning | Curious | Communication | Down | |

# GEMINI

Geminis are the most fluid talkers in the Zodiac. What thought occurs in the mind is usually verbalized on the tongue. This is a very social Sign. These people love to be involved in social gatherings. They are the butterflies of the Zodiac. They love to collect thoughts and ideas. They like to talk about the data they collect. This is the most versatile of the mutable Signs. They can almost do and think two different things at the same time. They have a need for more than one major interest in life. This is the most mentally active of all the Signs. Because of the constant mental activity, Geminis need some quiet time each day to wind down.

Since Gemini is the natural ruler of the Third House, Geminis enjoy all forms of communication — radio, TV, newspapers, magazines, telephone, etc. Because of this, they are usually well informed and make interesting conversationalists. Being quick witted, they are often witty as well. They like to make short trips and run errands. They like the sociability of these activities. Education is important to them. These are the people who really enjoy going to school. Because of their desire to touch so many different things, they can become too involved with surface matters and can lack depth. They must watch the tendency to be always on stage.

While not being particularly materialistic, Geminis are often attracted to money because they associate it with power. They're not too free with their own money, however.

Debbie Kempton Smith, in her book, Secret's From A Star Gazer's Notebook, says of Gemini men that even in old age they see themselves as cute little boys. Geminis age gracefullly, and tend to retain a youthful attitude toward life.

I have several close Gemini friends. They are wonderful assets at parties. When you're mixing new people at a party, there's nothing quite like a Gemini to keep the conversation flowing.

# CANCER

Approximate Dates:
June 22 - July 22
Symbol: The Crab

Quality: Cardinal
Element: Water
Ruling Planet: Moon

| HAS: | IS: | LIKES: | NEEDS: | THE MOST: |
|---|---|---|---|---|
| Domestic talent | Nurturing | Home | Security | Tenacious |
| Management | Cautious | Family | Love | |
| ability | Moody | Country | To protect | |
| Good memory | Emotional | Food | | |
| Sensitivity | | | | |

# CANCER

The symbol of Cancer is the crab. This is a wonderful visual association of the Sign. The crab carries its home on its back. Cancer people would do this if it were possible. Home and family are vitally important to Cancers. These people enjoy domestic things. A strong Cancer influence in a Chart can indicate a talent for cooking and/or a good sense of design in home furnishings. Not only is family dear to a Cancer person, but country as well. Cancers are patriotic.

This is the second money-making Sign. Cancers can hang on to money as well as people. This is the most tenacious of all the Signs. Since Cancer is ruled by the Moon, and the Moon is ever changing, Cancer people are subject to moods. This is the moodiest Sign, but most Cancers resent being called moody. Because they are so sensitive and have deep feelings, they do not like criticism. If you want variety in your life, marry a Cancer. Cancers are very sensitive to the phases of the Moon, so as the Moon changes Signs approximately every 2 1/2 days, your spouse could change personality moods every 2 1/2 days too!

The surroundings of a Cancer person are tremendously important. They would rather stay home than stay in an unattractive place when they travel. My youngest son has a Cancer Sun and Moon. When he was in college, he was a "resident assistant" in a dormitory in his sophomore year, which meant he had a private room and free room and board. But he didn't like the atmosphere of the cement block dormitory room, so he took another job for the next two years. He had to work many more hours, but he moved into a nice apartment with a beautiful view of a lake. He and the other Cancer people I know are good cooks. They like to entertain with small dinner parties at home. Two loves of a Cancer — good food and home.

This is the strongest nurturing Sign. Cancer people like to "mother" you. They naturally think of the welfare of the people they're with. Whenever you visit the home of a Cancer person (Sun, Moon or Ascendant), you will be offered some nourishment, or a refreshing drink — even if you've dropped by unexpectedly. The Cancer Moon people are good at listening to your problems. While Cancers in general are sensitive and caring, they don't reveal much of their inner selves. When they become emotionally vulnerable, they go within their shell.

Cancer people are good money managers. They usually have natural business ability and good executive instincts. They often prefer to work on their own. Because security is important to them, they seldom gamble.

LEO

Approximate Dates:                          Quality: Fixed
July 23 - August 22                         Element: Fire
Symbol: The Lion                            Ruling Planet: Sun

| HAS: | IS: | LIKES: | NEEDS: | THE MOST: |
|------|-----|--------|--------|-----------|
| Leadership ability | Creative | To be center of attention | To be own boss | Creative |
| Self confidence | Dramatic | To skip routine details | Pleasure | |
| Dignity | Generous | | | |
| Personal magnetism | Proud | | | |

# LEO

Leo is the most creative Sign. Leos want to create children of their bodies or their minds. They are the most original and creative gift-givers in the Zodiac. Leo is one of the actor's Signs. The type of actor represented would be the strong, dynamic type with a very dramatic, magnetic style. The symbol of Leo is the lion. The lion is the king of the animal world. Leos have a natural nobility and seldom lose their dignity. Since Leo is the natural ruler of the Fifth House, there is an enjoyment of entertainment, parties, games, etc. Leos usually relate well with children because of this House connection.

The Sun rules Leo, and it is the "boss" of the Solar System. So, Leos have leadership ability and like to be in positions of authority. This is a Sign of strong willpower.

Leos have great executive ability and they are very ambitious. There are many women with a Leo Sun or Ascendant who reach high levels of management in the business world. They work best where they manage a department, or where they work on their own. Since they are so creative, Leos usually like to work with their own ideas instead of someone else's. They will work "with" people rather than "for" people. While they are hard workers, they dislike routine and menial tasks. Their feeling of royalty often inclines them to let other people wait on them. So they tend to sit, while your Virgo friends automatically pitch in and help!

Since the ruler of Leo is the Sun, Leos love to be in the spotlight. As the Sun is the center of the Solar System, Leos like to be the center of their groups, whether social or business. They like people to "orbit around them." Leos must guard against a tendency to be too domineering or bossy.

Leos are usually "big-hearted" and generous. They often give too much in love relationships. Leo rules the heart. The Leos I know are fun to be with, and this is even more evident with Leo on the Ascendant. Leo is the least extroverted of all the Fire and Air Signs. Leos do not like deceit or pettiness.

# VIRGO

Approximate Dates:
August 23 - September 22
Symbol: The Virgin

Quality: Mutable
Element: Earth
Ruling Planet: Mercury

| HAS: | IS: | LIKES: | NEEDS: | THE MOST: |
|---|---|---|---|---|
| Great attention to detail | Hard working | To work undisturbed | To apply knowledge | Unassuming |
| Analytical ability | Skeptical | To serve and help | To be appreciated | |
| Self-control | Practical | To criticize | Good hygiene | |
| | Craftsman | | | |

## VIRGO

Virgos are the worker bees of the Zodiac. They love to apply what they know to service. These people are highly analytical with incredible attention to detail. They like to work behind the scenes where their work will not be interrupted. They are often quiet and shy. My students have heard me say many times that my great wish in life is to have a Virgo secretary. I couldn't find a more efficient and reliable Sign. When I once had therapy on a torn back muscle, the physical therapist had such unbelievable devotion and skill in her work that I asked if she were a Virgo. Her surprised answer was "Yes, how did you know?" Virgos are often talented at crafts. They like to make things that are beautiful and practical.

Virgos possess a love of precision and orderliness, a sense of duty and honesty. They dislike excess and extremes; therefore, they are usually reserved. Because of this, they sometimes fail to reach their full potential as they are not good at promoting themselves.

It's usually easy to spot someone with a strong Virgo influence (either Sun, Ascendant or Moon in Virgo). My husband has a Virgo Moon. On many occasions, he has clipped a loose thread on my collar or brushed lint off my shoulder while still giving me a "hello hug." Virgos are so good at spotting what's wrong, and they have such a need to make it right, that it can be disconcerting. When I tell my husband what I think is a new, terrific idea, I have learned to say, "Please tell me what you like about it first before you tell me what's wrong with it!" I do want to benefit from his keen powers of observation, but I don't want to always hear what's wrong up front. This is a tendency that Virgos should be aware of. They have such a compulsion to make everything right that the first thing they spot is what's wrong. This critical tendency is also apparent where Virgo is found on the Third House Cusp of communication. They are wonderful, helpful people. You never have to ask a Virgo to help — they automatically pitch in. The Virgos that I have taught in astrology classes are always the ones who would immediately gather the tea cups and clear the table at the end of class.

This Sign tends to produce fussy digestions. Virgos pay the greatest attention to health and hygiene. With their strong desire for perfection, they tend not to marry too young. In fact, there are more single women with Venus in Virgo because "no one can quite come up to their perfection!" Virgos can moderate their passions. They possess discipline and control. Many do not overeat, or drink. Virgos have a low divorce rate because of their cautious decisions in choosing a spouse. It's a well-modulated Sign.

# LIBRA

Approximate Dates:                              Quality: Cardinal
September 23 - October 22                       Element: Air
Symbol: The Scales                              Ruling Planet: Venus

| HAS: | IS: | LIKES: | NEEDS: | THE MOST: |
|------|-----|--------|--------|-----------|
| Diplomacy | Charming | Harmony | Partner | Balanced |
| Social ability | Popular | To relate with | To be important | |
| Appreciate of beauty | Slow to make decisions | the public | Mental stimulation | |
| | Friendly | To negotiate | | |

# LIBRA

The most important thing in the life of a Libra is a partner. These are the people who are aware of the opposite sex from kindergarten on. They need the other person to feel complete. This is the most harmonious Sign. It is one of the two most popular Signs.

The symbol of the scales is very good, as Libra is the most balanced of all the Signs. Libras are well liked. Libras constantly strive for balance because they want to be popular. They love the lime light and like to be important socially. They are naturally diplomatic. These are the public relations people of the Zodiac. Since the ruling Planet is Venus, Libras are often attractive, especially when this is the Rising Sign. They have an intellectual appreciation of beauty in contrast to Taurus (also ruled by Venus) where the attraction to beauty is more sensual.

Because of their need for a partner, Libras are usually interested in relationships and psychology. They make fine judges because of their ability to see both sides of every issue. This makes them slow and deliberate in making decisions. This can be a handicap when it affects their daily living. During my work as an interior designer, the only client I ever gave up was a Libra, who couldn't make up her mind on anything in a normal time span! The drawback of this Sign is that a Libra can be deceitful.

The one quality that has always surprised me in Libras is their lack of flexibility when their plans are changed. These sweet, social beings can really get bent out of shape when things don't go as expected, or arrangements are changed after the original agreement. This seems to throw their "scales" or "equilibrium" off balance. Their desire for balance and harmony can affect them physically, causing them to have an upset stomach during times of great stress.

Libra is the most romantic of all the Signs. If I had to use only one word to describe a Libra, the word would be charming. When the Libra Sun is prominent in the Chart, the charm is even more pronounced. The most charming couple I know both have prominent Libra Suns.

# SCORPIO

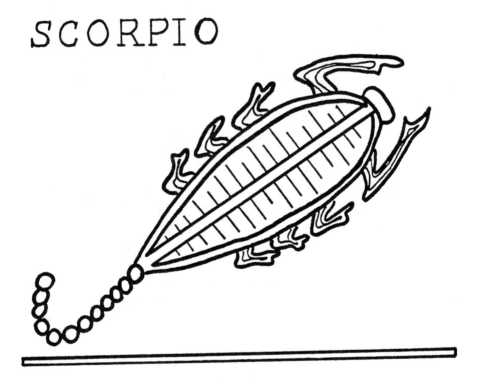

Approximate Dates:                          Quality: Fixed
October 23 - November 21                     Element: Water
Symbol: The Scorpion                         Ruling Planet: Pluto

| HAS: | IS: | LIKES: | NEEDS: | THE MOST: |
|------|-----|--------|--------|-----------|
| Tremendous | Intense | Secrets | Total self | Powerful |
| Reserve | Introspective | Hidden things | understanding | |
| Strength | Incisive | Sex (expressed | To give practical | |
| Perception | Never | or hidden) | help | |
| | superficial | To maneuver things | | |

# SCORPIO

This is the in-depth Sign. Scorpios are never content with surface appearances. Scorpio is the most intense Sign in the Zodiac. These people have powerful emotions. This Sign has the greatest swing between the high and low expression of its potential. It's often said, "Don't make an enemy of a Scorpio." And that includes a person with a Scorpio Ascendant. They are fighters who never surrender. The symbol of Scorpio is the scorpion. The scorpion does not naturally attack, but uses its stinger in self defense. It is the only animal that can kill itself, by stinging itself with its tail, which it would do rather than let another animal kill it.

Scorpios love to investigate and get to the bottom of things. They like you to tell them about yourself, but they like to be mysterious themselves. You have to try to figure them out. The better you are at this, the more they'll enjoy you. They're quick to analyze other people's weaknesses, and use this to their own advantage. This Sign has great interest in sex. This interest can have a natural expression, or it can by suppressed, but it's there, nevertheless. They are interested in all matters connected to the Eighth House. They are frequently early bloomers in their careers. This is also true when Scorpio is on the Ascendant.

Because of this concern with Eighth House matters, Scorpios make good psychologists. They love to probe beneath the surface. They are fearless in their desire to understand themselves. Since they are concerned about life and death, they often make good surgeons. Scorpio is a Water Sign, so these people are sensitive and caring. But they don't just give handouts. They'll help you learn to help yourself.

The Scorpios I know have a sexiness about them — either sexy eyes or voice, or both. Scorpios must be careful to control their egos and guard against any tendency to arrogance, rudeness or aloofness. Scorpios have a subtlety that makes them intriguing. Since this is the most powerful Sign, Scorpios have tremendous willpower.

# SAGITTARIUS

Approximate Dates:
November 22 - December 21
Symbol:  The Centaur/Archer

Quality:  Mutable
Element:  Fire
Ruling Planet:  Jupiter

| HAS: | IS: | LIKES: | NEEDS: | THE MOST: |
|------|-----|--------|--------|-----------|
| Enthusiasm | Friendly | To explore | Freedom | Mentally and |
| Love of learning | Cheerful | (mentally and | Independence | physically |
| Optimism | Talkative | physically) | To be on the | active in |
| Sense of fun | Honest | Philosophy | move | combination |
|  |  | Straightforward |  |  |
|  |  | approach |  |  |

# SAGITTARIUS

Cheerful, enthusiastic, friendly, outgoing and talkative are words most often used to describe a Sagittarian. While Aries is the most physically active Sign, and Gemini the most mentally active Sign, Sagittarius is the most physically and mentally active Sign in combination. These people are usually the athletes of the Zodiac. They love the out-of-doors and outdoor sports. They enjoy walking and often tennis and horseback riding. They are also the perpetual students of the Zodiac and usually enjoy learning throughout their lives.

Like their symbol, the Centaur-Archer, Sagittarians love to gallop off to pursue arrows in different directions and explore things. They enjoy Ninth House matters, and like to investigate philosophies, and then tell people which ones are valid. They often have more than one career in a lifetime, as they like to achieve a pinnacle and then move on to something else. They sometimes work at two different careers simultaneously. This can also occur when Sagittarius is on the Midheaven. They must guard against scattering their energy.

This is considered the most truthful of all the Signs. This quality can get the Sagittarian in trouble. The honesty can be too blunt at times and they can hurt people's feelings without realizing it. This bluntness is intended to be helpful and never unkind. But this directness can be too powerful for some people to handle. They have natural drive that causes them to go right to the heart of the matter. If someone deserves "a put-down" no one can do it better, faster, or more directly than a Sagittarian. Their arrows go straight to the mark. While they are very honest, they sometimes like to use exaggeration, deliberately and obviously, in describing things to make them more colorful and fun.

Most Sagittarians love to travel. They have all their cylinders going when meeting new people and visiting new places. They dislike routine, and love freedom.

Sagittarian women are not fond of domestic chores unless there is a strong Cancer influence in the Chart. They make wonderful hostesses, however. No one makes you feel more welcome than a Sagittarian. As children, the Sagittarians are called "the sunshine children of the Zodiac."

This is the most extroverted of all the Signs. It is also considered the luckiest Sign because of its Jupiter rulership. The luck stems from their incredible powers of positive thinking. They bring good things into their lives by constantly "programming" for them — naturally. Even in life's darkest moments, luck seems to arrive just in time.

# CAPRICORNNS

| Approximate Dates: | Quality: Cardinal |
|---|---|
| December 22 - January 19 | Element: Earth |
| Symbol: The Mountain Goat | Ruling Planet: Saturn |

| HAS: | IS: | LIKES: | NEEDS: | THE MOST: |
|---|---|---|---|---|
| Self-discipline | Tactful | Achievement | Recognition | Goal |
| Integrity | Serious | To converse | To be best | oriented |
| Reliability | Ambitious | Rules and | at a skill | |
| Perseverance | Cautious | regulations | To organize | |
| | | Wit | | |

# CAPRICORN

Capricorn is the Sign of the conservator. These people are the original recyclers in the Zodiac. They have natural reserve. They don't usually talk about themselves. Their most pronounced characteristics include perseverance, ambition, strong concentration, analytical ability, natural business sense and efficiency. They are reliable, practical, objective, prone to worry and clever in emergencies.

They are one of the longest-lived of all the Signs. They know this innately, and they work long and hard at becoming financially secure, as they do not want to be dependent on anyone else in old age. The symbol of the mountain goat is excellent, as this goat is very sure-footed as it makes its way up the mountainside. The Capricorn makes a slow, but steady, ascent up the ladder of success. They have great need for security, independence and prestige.

While most Capricorns are very serious, the ones I know all have a good sense of humor and are frequently witty. They seem to develop a sense of fun as they grow older. Success in this life is terribly important to Capricorns. Their philosophy is attuned to material things. Some Capricorns tend not to marry when they are very young since their careers are so important. In fact, Capricorn women think their professions are more important than their home lives. This is the third of the three money making Signs in the Zodiac. When Capricorn is on the Ascendant, there can be a strong tendency toward pessimism. This is the Sign that has to guard against melancholy feelings. Capricorns are usually calm, cool and collected. A Capricorn friend of mine is a wonderful example of this Sign. She is hard working, diligent, very witty and a great conservator. If she makes hors d'oeuvres
that call for bread squares ith the crusts cut off, she'll freeze the crusts, rather than throw them away, until she can think of another appetizer to make using the crusts!

This is one of two Ascending Signs that produces big, beautiful eyes. Capricorns have a great need to be appreciated also.

# AQUARIUS

Approximate Dates:
January 20 - February 18
Symbol: The Water Bearer

Quality: Fixed
Element: Air
Ruling Planet: Uranus

| HAS: | IS: | LIKES: | NEEDS: | THE MOST: |
|------|-----|--------|--------|-----------|
| Generosity | Unselfish | Unconventional | Stimulation in | Tolerant |
| Detachment | Inventive | people and | work | |
| Ingenuity | Social | things | To help people | |
| Independence | Humanitarian | Truth | in general | |
| | | To investigate | | |

# AQUARIUS

This is the Sign of the humanitarian. Its symbol of the water bearer is particularly appropriate. In Rudyard Kipling's poem Gunga Din, the water bearer is the central hero. Gunga Din carries water to the battle-worn soldiers, with little concern for his own welfare. The Aquarian reaches out to help people in need. They have great compassion and sympathy. Yet, since this is an Air Sign, Aquarians are emotionally detached. Because of this detachment, they are able to work with needy or psychologically disturbed people without being emotionally drained.

Aquarians have several easily recognized traits. First of all, they are not snobbish. They do not make any class distinctions. They enjoy people from all walks of life and all colors and creeds. Aquarians are extremely open-minded and accepting of the differences in other people. Secondly, they enjoy being with groups of friends — an Eleventh House connection where Aquarius is the natural ruler. Aquarian women like to have friends of the opposite sex even after they are married — they think of them as their pals. They also have a pronounced interest in new and unusual things in contrast to Capricorns. With Uranus as the ruling Planet, Aquarians have ability in science, math or astrology. This is a very inventive Sign. When Uranus is extremely prominent in a Natal Chart, it can be an indicator of great ability as an inventor, scientist, or astrologer.

There is usually pronounced ability in problem solving. This intellectual talent is apparent in either technical or theoretical fields. A friend who is a double Aquarian, with a First House Aquarian Sun, and Aquarius rising, uses the theoretical side of this talented Sign. While doing advanced studies in theology, she is the most open-minded, accepting and caring friend imaginable.

While Aquarius is one of the two most popular Signs, Aquarians can be solitary people. They like groups of friends, but seldom have close intimate friendships. They usually have good dispositions. Since Uranus is the revolutionary Planet, Aquarians can rebel against tradition and convention. Freedom is very important to them. They like independence.

# PISCES

Approximate Dates:
February 19 - March 20
Symbol: The Fish

Quality: Mutable
Element: Water
Ruling Planet: Neptune

| HAS: | IS: | LIKES: | NEEDS: | THE MOST: |
|---|---|---|---|---|
| Depth of feeling | Sensitive | The arts | Some quiet time | Imaginative |
| Compassion | Impression- | Spirituality | each day | |
| Charm | able | To be devoted | To help the | |
| Humor | Sympathetic | | unfortunate | |
| | Easy-going | | | |

# PISCES

The last Sign in the Zodiac is Pisces. This is the kindest, most gentle and the most intuitive of all the Signs. Like their symbol, the fish, Pisces people seem to have a gracefulness about them. They seem to glide through life. This is especially noticeable when Pisces is on the Ascendant. Pisces like to see the beauty in the world. Many Pisces people have a great dislike of news, TV shows, or films that show the low elements of life. They prefer soft, beautiful scenes instead of harsh realism. They like to view life through rose-colored glasses.

There is a great sensitivity to, and appreciation of, the fine arts. The greatest number of musicians are born during the Pisces Sun Sign period. There are also many artists and photographers with this Sign by Sun or Ascendant. Neptune, the ruling Planet of Pisces, is usually very prominent in the Natal Charts of actors and actresses. Pisces is one of the three Signs of the actor. The Pisces type of actor is not the dynamic Sagittarius type, or the dramatic Leo type, but more the quiet, deep-feeling actor. Robert Redford has a Pisces Ascendant.

This is also the most sympathetic Sign. Pisces people are often drawn to work in hospitals or other institutions where caring for people is important. There is a spiritual quality in most Pisces. When Pisces is on the Ascendant, the eyes are usually large, beautiful and sad.

The biggest drawback of this Sign is a lack of willpower. Unless there is strength in the Chart elsewhere, there can be a dependency on drugs or alcohol. There can be a desire for escapism. Neptune deals with illusion. The Pisces symbol of the fish tied together, but swimming in two different directions, shows the Pisces pull toward spirituality, or escapism. The free will of mankind allows the Piscean to choose the direction.

Pisces people are so psychic and intuitive that they almost "photograph scenes" as they go through life. Their deep impressionability allows them to be able to visualize a room after they have just walked through it once. This is an extremely imaginative Sign. Because the Pisceans pick up other people's vibrations so easily, it is necessary for them to have some quiet time alone every day. They must have a chance to let their batteries recharge. Pisces is the weakest physical Sign when it's on the Ascendant. These people simply "run out of gas." When this happens, they need to take a short rest.

This is the Sign of the martyr. Pisceans will sacrifice themselves for someone else, or some belief. They can also develop a martyr complex if the Piscean doesn't have the success he or she wants.

# THE GROUPINGS OF THE SIGNS

There are three important groupings of the twelve Zodiac Signs. They can serve as a wonderful short-cut to remembering characteristics of the different Signs. I explain this when I'm teaching by saying it is as if you are arranging the same number of people in the class in different ways. For example, I could group according to sex, putting the males together and the females together. Then I could regroup according to hair color (regardless of sex), putting brunettes in one group, blondes in another, redheads in a third and gray-haired people in a fourth group. A third group could be assembled according to eye color (regardless of sex or hair color), putting blue eyed people in one group, green in another and brown in another group. It's the same assemblage of people, but they're grouped three different ways. Let's look at the Sun Signs in three different groups:

## Group One:  Active/Passive Signs
## The Zodiac Divided by Twos

The Signs are first divided into active or passive Signs. These are also called masculine and feminine. It has to do with energy, not sexuality. Think of the plus and minus marks on batteries. It takes both types to produce energy.

The active and passive (or receptive) Signs alternate through the Zodiac. Aries, Gemini, Leo, Libra, Sagittarius and Aquarius are active Signs. These are extroverted people. Taurus, Cancer, Virgo, Scorpio, Capricorn and Pisces are the passive Signs. These are the more introverted Signs.

In 1978, English astrologer, Jeff Mayo, had a paper published in The American Journal of Social Psychology, Volume 105. The article was jointly written with Professor Hans Eysenck, Director of the Department of Psychology at the Institute of Psychiatry in London. The paper was based on two research studies. Jeff Mayo set out to prove conclusively "that these two basic attitudes of extroversion-introversion can be associated with alternate Zodiacal Signs." He used the Institute's computer for the data analysis on his first study of 1,795 questionnaires. For the second study, the universally recognized E.P.I. (Eysenck Personality Inventory) was used. This inventory measures two dimensions of personality: extroversion-introversion and emotional stability-instability. 2,324 samples were used in the second study from people of all ages from all over the world. Both studies produced a saw-tooth graph showing extremes between the alternating Sun Signs. The most extroverted Sign was Sagittarius, followed by Aries. There was a drop-off to the next level of extroversion where Aquarius, Libra and Gemini ran a close race. Leo was the least extroverted of the Fire and Air Signs.

The Earth and Water Signs all fell below the mean. Pisces and Virgo showed the greatest tendency to introversion, with Taurus close behind. Next came Capricorn, then Scorpio and finally Cancer, which was the lease introverted of this group.

In the March 2, 1977 issue of the London Evening Standard, there was an article about this research which was distributed world-wide by the Associated Press. Professor Eysenck was quoted, "...when the results were put through the computer, the predicted relations between personality and birthdate did in fact come out very clearly.

"I must admit that this was a great surprise to me.. my instinctive skepticism and dislike of anything mystical had led me to expect unrelieved failure from any investigations of astrological predictions. To find some solid fact in the astrological field was surprising and not entirely welcome...

"...so far all we have are these mysterious, but to me at least fascinating, glimpses of aspects of reality which scientists so far have refused to look at. Perhaps our arrogance has been misplaced: there may indeed be more things in heaven and Earth than we have dreamt of!"

Jeff Mayo discusses this study at length in his book, How To Teach Yourself Astrology.

## Group Two: The Elements
## The Zodiac Divided By Fourths

The second grouping is by Element, which indicates temperament. These are the four Elements that make up the Earth's atmosphere: Fire, Earth, Air and Water. There are three Signs in each Element. It looks as if you are dividing a pie into thirds when you look at the Elements.

The Fire Signs are: Aries, Leo and Sagittarius. The Earth Signs are: Taurus, Virgo and Capricorn. The Air Signs are: Gemini, Libra and Aquarius. The Water Signs are: Cancer, Scorpio and Pisces. The groupings by Element are called triplicities.

| ELEMENT | MEMORY ASSOCIATION | CHARACTERISTICS |
|---|---|---|
| Fire | Fiery | Assertive |
| Aries | Warm | Enthusiastic |
| Leo | | Outgoing |
| Sagittarius | | Leadership ability |
| Earth | Earthy | Reliable |
| Taurus | Down to Earth | Practical |
| Virgo | | Realistic |
| Capricorn | | Managers |
| Air | Airy | Mental Activity |
| Gemini | Light touch | Communicator |
| Libra | | Social |
| Aquarius | | Detached |
| Water | Watery emotions | Emotional |
| Cancer | Tears of joy or sorrow | Sensitive |
| Scorpio | | Intuitive |
| Pisces | | Receptive |

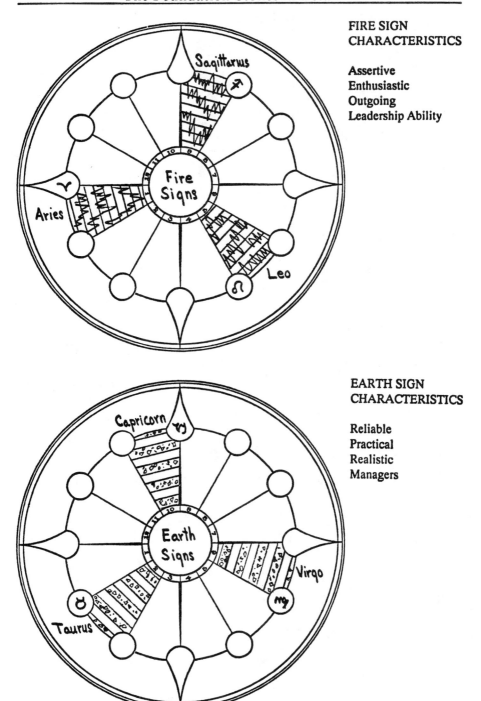

FIRE SIGN
CHARACTERISTICS

Assertive
Enthusiastic
Outgoing
Leadership Ability

EARTH SIGN
CHARACTERISTICS

Reliable
Practical
Realistic
Managers

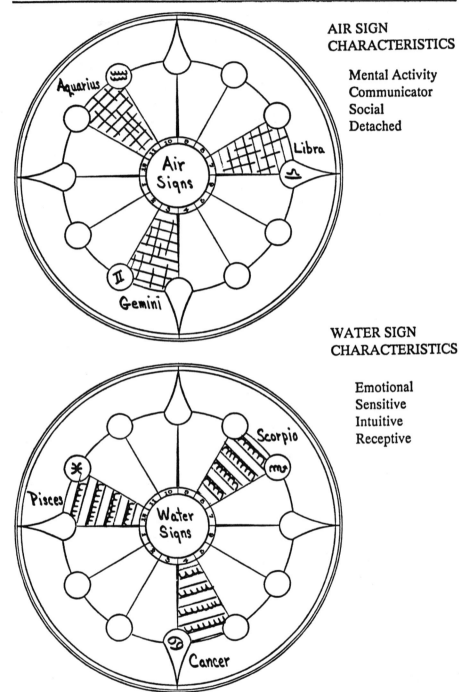

**AIR SIGN CHARACTERISTICS**

Mental Activity
Communicator
Social
Detached

**WATER SIGN CHARACTERISTICS**

Emotional
Sensitive
Intuitive
Receptive

# Group Three:  The Qualities
## The Zodiac Divided By Thirds

The third major grouping of the Signs is by Quality, which shows type of action. There are four Signs in each of the three Qualities, so it looks as if you are dividing the pie into fourths. The qualities are: Cardinal, Fixed and Mutable. The Cardinal Signs, marking the change of seasons, are: Aries, Cancer, Libra and Capricorn. The Fixed Signs are: Taurus, Leo, Scorpio and Aquarius. The Mutable Signs are: Gemini, Virgo, Sagittarius and Pisces. The grouping by Quality is called the quadruplicities.

| QUALITY | CHARACTERISTICS | MEMORY ASSOCIATION |
| --- | --- | --- |
| Cardinal | Dynamic | Change of season or |
| Aries | Initiative | the football |
| Cancer | Active | quarterback |
| Libra | Executive ability | |
| Capricorn | Initiates change | |
| | | |
| Fixed | Stable | The oak tree or the |
| Taurus | Stubborn | football lineman |
| Leo | Planner | |
| Scorpio | Powerful | |
| Aquarius | Resistant to change | |
| | | |
| Mutable | Adaptable | The willow tree or the |
| Gemini | Flexible | football running |
| Virgo | Versatile | back |
| Sagittarius | Quick in emergencies | |
| Pisces | Responsive to change | |

# THE QUALITIES

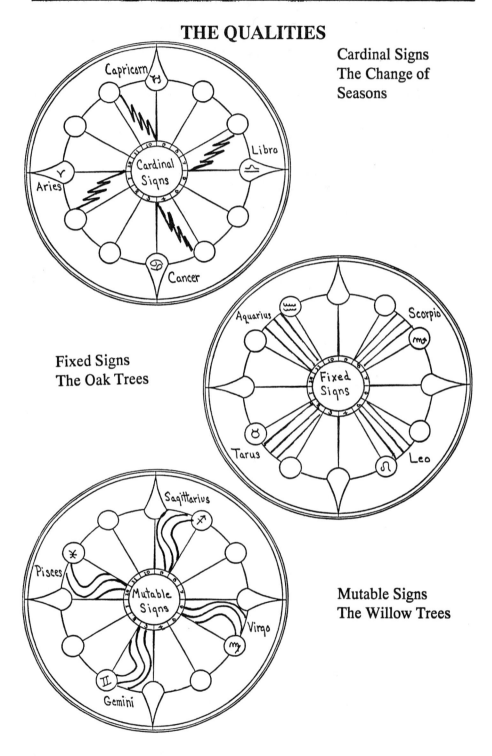

Cardinal Signs
The Change of
Seasons

Fixed Signs
The Oak Trees

Mutable Signs
The Willow Trees

Many years ago, I read a description of how to view the Elements as they function together. I cannot remember where I read it, so I cannot give a credit line to the astrologer. It was suggested that the Air Signs are idea people; the Fire Signs are the ones who get people excited about the idea; the Earth Signs will do the work; and the Water Signs will take care of the project after the work is completed. I have taken this idea a step further to help visualize the interaction of the Elements:

| Element | Function | Result |
|---------|----------|--------|
| Air | Idea | Need for a community orphanage |
| Fire | Get people interested | Raise funds to build the orphanage |
| Earth | Plan and design the building | Build the orphanage |
| Water | Emotional | Care for the children and the building |

When there is a lack of a particular Element in a Chart, meaning no Planets, or only one Planet in a particular Element, it indicates the following:

| Missing Element | Lacking |
|-----------------|---------|
| Fire | Enthusiasm, Self esteem |
| Earth | Practicality, Common sense |
| Air | Detachment |
| Water | Emotional depth |

# THE ELEMENTS AND QUALITIES IN OVERVIEW

The Elements and Qualities are a very important part of astrology. You should memorize them. Start by first memorizing the Element of your Sun Sign. Next, memorize the Element of your Ascendant. Then, memorize the Element of your Moon. After you know these, begin to memorize the Qualities of your Sun, Ascendant and Moon.

Now, here's "the biggie" — a shortcut to learning descriptions of the twelve Signs. If you are a Leo Sun Sign, for example, you first know that you are a Fire Sign. What are Fire Sign people? They're fiery, enthusiastic, outgoing and leaders. Leo is also a Fixed Sign. Fixed Sign people are stable, persistent, determined and stubborn. There is only one Fire Sign that is also a Fixed Sign. So, by combining the descriptions of Fire and Fixed, you have described a Leo. So, memorizing the Elements and Qualities gives you an instant description of all twelve Signs of the Zodiac. If you're at a party and people find out you're "into astrology" and ask you to tell them about themselves, you just plug into your "Element/Quality computer." If that person is a Libra, you first use the key words for Air Signs. Next, you combine that with the descriptive words for Cardinal Signs. Libra is the only Air Sign that is also a Cardinal Sign. If a person has Virgo for his or her Sun Sign, you would use the key words for Earth Signs and Mutable Signs. Virgo is the only Earth Sign that is also a Mutable Sign. The three Signs in each Element are always in separate Qualities. For a Cancer person you would use the words to describe a Water Sign and then a Cardinal Sign. Cancer is the only Water Sign that is also a Cardinal Sign.

# THE ELEMENTS AND QUALITIES

| THE SIGN | THE QUALITY | THE ELEMENT | IN COMBINATION |
|----------|-------------|-------------|----------------|
| Aries | Cardinal | Fire | Cardinal/Fire |
| Taurus | Fixed | Earth | Fixed/Earth |
| Gemini | Mutable | Air | Mutable/Air |
| Cancer | Cardinal | Water | Cardinal/Water |
| Leo | Fixed | Fire | Fixed/Fire |
| Virgo | Mutable | Earth | Mutable/Earth |
| Libra | Cardinal | Air | Cardinal/Air |
| Scorpio | Fixed | Water | Fixed/Water |
| Sagittarius | Mutable | Fire | Mutable/Fire |
| Capricorn | Cardinal | Earth | Cardinal/Earth |
| Aquarius | Fixed | Air | Fixed/Air |
| Pisces | Mutable | Water | Mutable/Water |

# PLANETARY RULERSHIPS

Each Sign of the Zodiac has a Planet that is called the Ruler. It is the Planet whose energy functions most naturally in that individual Sign. There is a connection between the Planet and the Sign that helps in memorizing the Rulerships. The Rulerships are a very important part of basic astrology and they should be committed to memory. There are twelve Signs and only ten Planets, so two of the Planets have to do double duty.

| SIGN | RELATIONSHIP | PLANETARY RULER |
|------|-------------|-----------------|
| Aries | Energy | Mars |
| Taurus | Tangible beauty | Venus |
| Gemini | Communicating | Mercury |
| Cancer | Emotional nurturing | Moon |
| Leo | Creativity/Life force | Sun |
| Virgo | Mental purity | Mercury |
| Libra | Harmony, Love | Venus |
| Scorpio | In-depth power | Pluto |
| Sagittarius | The jovial Sign and Planet | Jupiter |
| Capricorn | Responsibility/Structure | Saturn |
| Aquarius | The new and unusual | Uranus |
| Pisces | The mystical Sign/Planet | Neptune |

# THE PLANETS
# THE ASTRONOMY OF ASTROLOGY

| PLANETS | ORBIT AROUND THE SUN | ROTATION ON AXIS | DISTANCE FROM SUN |
|---|---|---|---|
| Sun | | | (39 Million from Earth) |
| Moon | | | (240,000 from Earth) |
| Mercury | 86 Days | 59 Days | 36 Million |
| Venus | 225 Days | 243 Days | 67 Million |
| Mars | 687 Days | 24 Hr. 37 Min. | 142 Million |
| Jupiter | 12 Years | 9 Hr. 55 Min. | 484 Million |
| Saturn | 29.5 Years | 10 Hr. 39 Min. | 887 Million |
| Uranus | 84 Years | 16 to 28 Hr. | 1,784 Million |
| Neptune | 165 Years | 15 Hr. 40 Min. | 2,795 Million |
| Pluto | 248 Years | 6 Days | 3,675 Million |

* The World Book Encyclopedia

# THE ASTRONOMY OF ASTROLOGY

## THE DIAMETER OF THE PLANETS
### Relationship Of Their Sizes To Each Other*
### (Distances in Kilometers)

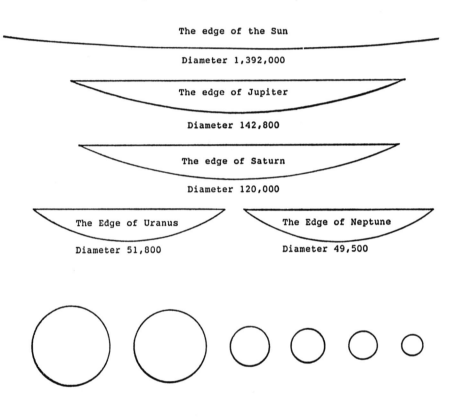

The edge of the Sun

Diameter 1,392,000

The edge of Jupiter

Diameter 142,800

The edge of Saturn

Diameter 120,000

The Edge of Uranus          The Edge of Neptune

Diameter 51,800              Diameter 49,500

| Planet: | Earth | Venus | Mars | Pluto | Mercury | Moon |
|---------|-------|-------|------|-------|---------|------|
| Diameter: | 12,756 | 12,104 | 6,787 | 5,800? | 4,880 | 3,476 |

* Astronomy: The Cosmic Journey
   William K. Hartman
   Dodsworth Publishing Company

# ASTROLOGICAL MEANING OF THE PLANETS

## THE SUN

The center of the Solar System is the Sun. It is also the major focus of astrology. It represents your life force, your will, your inner cord. It is the single most important point in your Chart. The Sign it falls in will describe your basic character. The Sun is called one of the two lights, or luminaries, in astrology. The Sun also governs your physical heart which is your life force. Its placement in your Chart is of tremendous importance, as an indicator of your life's thrust and goals.

## THE MOON

The Moon in astrology describes your emotional nature and your subconscious mind: the Sign that your Moon is in will indicate the type of emotional response you make instinctively. The influence of the Sign is not usually as apparent as the Sun or Ascendant Signs, because it functions beneath the surface. Where the Moon appears in your Chart will be where you have the strongest emotional attachment. You will receive your greatest emotional comfort in that area. The Moon is the second light, or luminary, after the Sun.

## THE ASCENDANT

The second-most important point in the Chart is the Ascendant. It is determined by the point on the eastern horizon at the moment of your birth. The Ascendant decribes the physical you and your outward personality. Aspects to it are very important and have great influence on your personality and physical well-being.

# MERCURY

In ancient mythology, Mercury was considered the messenger of the gods. In astrology, Mercury still plays the role of messenger, as it is the Planet of communication. By Sign placement, Mercury would describe the type of mind you have. Mercury represents our mental faculty and reasoning ability. The Aspects to Mercury in your Chart will give further information as to the workings of your mind. Mercury is often described as your microphone, so the memory association of antennae should help you identify Mercury. The house containing Mercury in your Chart would show the area of life that you like to talk about. Mercury is never more than 28 Degrees away from the Sun. So, Mercury would either be in the same Sign as your Sun, or in one of the two adjacent Signs of your Sun Sign.

# VENUS

The Planet Venus is the brightest and most beautiful Planet that we see without a telescope. It is called the "evening star" because it's seen just after sundown (unless it's on the other side of the Sun). Venus is never more that 48 Degrees from the Sun. In astrology, Venus represents beauty and love. Where Venus is positioned in your Chart will show the kinds of things you love. In the First House, Venus usually bestows good looks. In the Third House, Venus would indicate a love of communication. A Ninth House Venus could mean a love of foreign travel and/or books dealing with subjects of the higher mind. Venus rules money, beautiful art objects and decorative articles. The Sign that Venus falls in describes your type of sensuality and love nature. For example, Venus in Taurus would be very sensual. Venus in an Air Sign would be less physically demonstrative and the expression of love would be more mental.

# MARS

Mars represents energy — our physical energy and our ego energy. It's our offensive and defensive mechanism. It helps to remember its glyph by thinking of the circle as a shield (for protection) and the arrow as a spear (for aggression). When people are described as "having an ego problem," they often have some difficult Aspects to Mars. I've noticed that people with Mars in a Fire or Air Sign are assertive drivers, while most people with Mars in a Water Sign tend to be cautious drivers, and even timid drivers when Mars is in Pisces.

Mars shows the active part of your sexuality. It describes the aggressive part of your nature. In your Chart, the placement of Mars shows where you will put your energy drive, and often has a relationship to your work.

Mars is such a strong Planet that it can dominate the personality of a Chart when it is prominently placed and strongly Aspected. This is most often apparent when Mars is in a Fire Sign and can also occur when it appears in an Air Sign. (Fire and Air Signs are explained in the Sun Signs Chapter under "Groupings of the Signs"). Mars can also be a dominant quality combined with the Sun or Ascendant. A friend of mine has an Aquarian Sun with Mars Conjunct the Sun. She has pronounced Aries/Mars traits. She is tremendously energized, has reddish hair, and the assertive, take charge personality of an Aries.

## JUPITER

Jupiter is the Planet of expansion, and good fortune. It is the ruling Planet of the Ninth House which deals with abstract thought and distant travel of the mind or body. Because of this House connection it governs philosophy, religion, law and publishing. Wherever Jupiter is located by House in your Chart is where you will have good luck. It offers luck through the opportunities for growth and expansion in that area of your life. Jupiter is one of the two spiritual Planets, and there is often a spiritual connection with the way Jupiter is expressed in your Chart.

# SATURN

In nature, there is a rhythm for expansion and contraction. Just after Jupiter offers us expansion, Saturn brings contraction. Saturn is the Planet of structure and restriction. Saturn likes rules and regulations as do Capricorns — the Sign ruled or most closely connected to Saturn. It governs business, and often shows a personal business influence in the Chart. Saturn is called the teacher in astrology. It shows by House location where we will have the opportunity to learn, and where we can take on great responsibility. Wherever we take on responsibility in one area, we are restricted in our time for other things. If Saturn's restrictions in our lives are accepted willingly, we don't feel the burden of the Planet. The rings around Saturn serve as a visual reminder of its restriction. The nature of the House where Saturn lies will be developed slowly.

# URANUS

Just after Saturn makes us "toe the mark" along comes Uranus daring us to be different! Uranus is the only Planet whose axis is perpendicular to those of all the other Planets. A recent scientific report noted that Uranus, in certain configurations to other Planets, occurred during all the major earthquakes in the twentieth century. Uranus is the Planet of sudden change. It is the revolutionary Planet. It is the Planet of the inventor, or the scientist, or the astrologer when it is prominently placed in the Chart. Wherever Uranus falls in your Chart shows where you can use your ingenuity and march to your own drummer. It will be the area of life where you will feel most free, as Uranus is the Planet of freedom and revolution. Because of your feeling of freedom, you are able to let your creativity flow wherever Uranus is located.

Uranus was discovered by Sir William Herschel in 1781. He is considered to be perhaps the greatest observational astronomer who ever lived. He contributed greatly to the development of the telescope. The glyph for Uranus looks like an H for Herschel with a pendulum attached.

# NEPTUNE

The second spiritual Planet is Neptune. Neptune rules Pisces, the Sign of the fish. It deals with mystical matters. It also has an illusionary connotation. It helps to think of the way fish appear in water — as if there were a mysterious veil enveloping them. Where Neptune lies in your Chart is where you will seek the ideal. It can also indicate where you can be disillusioned. Neptune is also the Planet of the imagination. If it is strongly Aspected in your Chart, you should be highly imaginative.

The glyph for Neptune is represented as the trident which is traditionally shown in the hand of King Neptune who rules the seas. There is an easy memory association between the sea and the Sign which Neptune rules - Pisces, the fish.

# PLUTO

Since astrology is knowledge through observation, there is less known about the effects of Pluto (discovered in 1930) than any other Planet. In the years of observation, Pluto has shown a strong connection with the underworld. It represents the physical underworld of geology, mining and archaeology. It is also the Planet of the underworld of man's mind, as seen through psychology and psychiatry. And in some cases, it can represent the criminal underworld.

Pluto brings power to the area of your Chart by House location through regeneration. I use the memory association of P and L for the first two letters of the Planet and also for Sir Percival Lovell who discovered the Planet. The other memory association is the steam shovel, because Pluto represents death and rebirth through regeneration.

Percival Lovell began the calculations for Pluto in 1905. From this research Pluto was actually discovered 25 years later by Clyde Tombaugh. There is a special symbol for Pluto which looks like a chalice with a circle inside, but I think the P L is an easier symbol to remember.

# POSITION OF PLANETS IN THE NATAL CHART BY HOUSE LOCATION

SUN

Where you should focus your life achievements.

MOON

Where you have emotional attachment/Where you go for comfort.

MERCURY

What you like to talk about and think about.

VENUS

The kinds of things you love and enjoy.

MARS

The area of life where you put your physical energy.

JUPITER

Where you will have good luck through expansion.

SATURN

Where you take on the heaviest responsibility, and therefore feel restriction/Where there can be problems and delays.

URANUS

Where you will dare to be different, and march to your own drummer/Where you can use your ingenuity.

NEPTUNE

Where you seek the ideal in life/Where you find spiritual attachment and sometimes disillusionment.

PLUTO

Where you will find strength and power through regeneration.

# THE HOUSES/THE NATAL CHART

The Natal Chart is a map of the Solar System, by celestial longitude, at the moment of your birth. The center of the wheel, or circle, represents the city or place in which you were born. The Chart shows a circle of 360 Degrees, which is ringed by the 12 Constellations of the Zodiac.

Astrology is based on the astronomy of the Planets. It then interprets the Planets by Sign and House location, and the possible geometric relationships between the Planets. The result gives a psychological profile of the individual. Basic drives and emotional needs are shown, describing the personality and character.

When we talk about a horoscope (which means hour of birth), we are referring to the Natal Chart. The term Natal Chart, which means birth Chart, is the term used by astrologers.

The Natal Chart is two things in one. First, it is a picture or diagram of the Solar System at the moment of your birth — like a "freeze action shot" in photography. This view is from Earth, as seen from the city or town in which you were born, which is placed at the center of the Chart. The longitude and latitude of your birthplace is used, along with the time of the day and the time zone. Secondly, it is a circle, or wheel, divided into 12 areas, with time designated for 24 hours. Please note the hours as seen on the wheel in example. The Solar System map is laid on top of the astrological wheel. How it fits is determined by the exact time of birth.

If your were born at 1:37 P.M., the glyph representing your Sun Sign would appear in the Ninth House. The Houses are numbered near the center of the wheel in counter-clockwise order. If you were born at 7:23 P.M., the Sun would appear in the Fifth House. If you were born at 5:15 A.M., the Sun would be in the First House, and so on. The Houses are numbered 1 through 12, each designating a two-hour time span.

The Sun represents your basic character, your will, your inner core. It will be described by the Constellation Sign it falls in, and your basic drive will be indicated by the House in which it is located. It will be further colored by any geometric contacts made to it by other Planets (this will be explained in the chapter on Aspects).

The Chart is figured mathematically by celestial longitude. Astrology is based on the astronomy of the Planets, so it takes close to an hour of math to figure each Chart. The majority of professional astrologers use computers for the mathematical calculations. There are many different styles of astrological wheels. The one I have selected for this book is my personal preference because I find it visually very easy to read.*

The symbol for the Sun is a circle with a dot in the center. The symbol for the Moon looks like a crescent-shaped Moon. The symbol is placed closest to the outer circle. The Degree number follows the symbol in a direction toward the center of the circle, and finally the symbol, or glyph, for the Zodiac Sign is located closest to the center. Latitude is read first by Degree, and then by Minutes — such as 39° N 06 Minutes; longitude 84° W 31 Minutes for the city of Cincinnati. For San Diego, the latitude is 32° N 43 Minutes; longitude 117° W 9 Minutes.

* Chart Form: No. 5 - Macoy, Richmond, Virginia

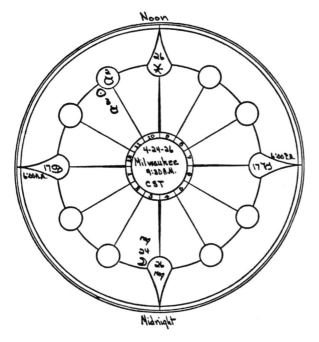

Milwaukee Chart A
9:30 A.M.
Sun in the 11th House
Moon in the 3rd House
in Virgo

Chart A is the birth time
of a man born in Milwau-
kee. Since he was born at
9:30 A.M., the Sun is in
Taurus, located in the
11th House which is the
time slot for 8:00 - 10:00
A.M. His Moon is in
Virgo in the 3rd House.

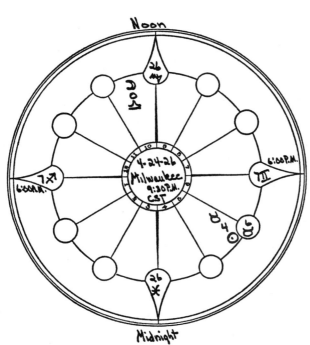

Milwaukee Chart B
9:30 P.M.
Sun in the 5th House
Moon in the 10th House
in Libra

Had the man been born
12 hours later, the Sun
would be in the 5th
House as seen in Chart B.
This is the House where
the time designation is
8:00 - 10:00 P.M. In this
Chart, the fast-moving
Moon has gone into a
new Sign at 0° of Libra,
and is located in the 10th
House.

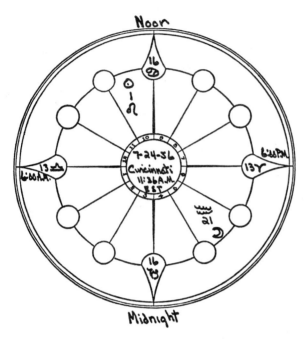

Cincinnati Chart A

The actual time of birth
for this man was 11:36
A.M. So the Sun at 1° of
Leo must be in the 10th
House. The House
designated time is 10:00
A.M. to 12 Noon.

Cincinnati Chart B

Chart B shows where the
Sun would be located in
the 8th House had the
man been born at 4:04
P.M. The Moon would
have moved 2° to 23°
Aquarius and would be
placed in the Third
House.

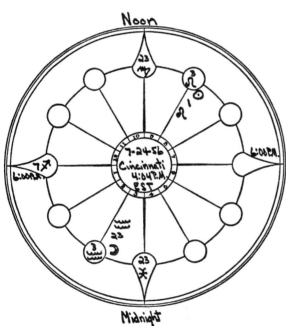

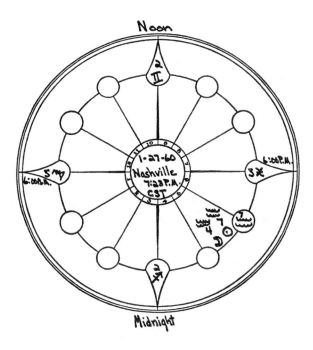

## Nashville Chart A

This young man was born at 7:23 P.M. The Sun at 7° Aquarius is shown here in the 5th House where the time designation is 8:00 - 10:00 P.M. The reason that his Sun is located in the 5th and not the 6th House is because Nashville is off true Sun time by 47 minutes.

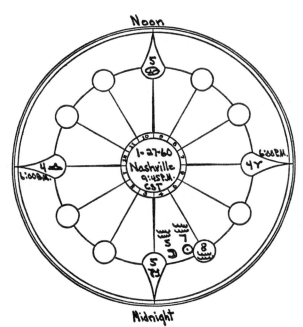

## Nashville Chart B

Chart B shows where his Sun and Moon would be had the man been born 2 hours and 22 minutes later. The Moon would have moved into 5° of Aquarius. Both the Sun and Moon would be placed in the 4th House of 10:00 P.M. - 12 Midnight time. Once again, the Sun would be in the 4th instead of the 5th House because of the true Sun time affecting the close position of the time between the Houses.

## QUICK REFERENCE FOR THE HOUSES

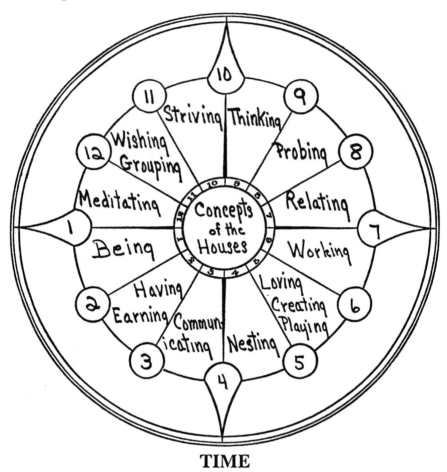

## TIME

Time has a tremendously important role to play in your Chart. To know what Sign was rising at the moment of your birth, you must have your birth time. This is often found on birth certificates. If it's not, check the family Bible, or record book or your baby book if you have one. A scrapbook might contain your birth announcement. One of my students had a silver baby cup with her date and time engraved on it. Another method for obtaining your time is getting a copy of your birth record from the hospital where you were born. You should call the hospital to see if they still have their records from the year you were born. If they do, send a money order for a copy of your birth record. This usually costs as much as a birth certificate.

If your time of birth can't be found, you can have a Solar Chart done. This Chart places the Sun at the Ascending point, and can be figured with the longitude and latitude of your birth place. A Solar Chart will give you a great deal of information. It will place all the Planets in the correct Signs and show their geometric relationship to each other. It cannot give your Ascendant, Midheaven, house location of your Planets, or the exact Degree of the Moon. There is a method of determining your time of birth called Rectification in astrology. This is explained in a later chapter.

When an astrologer calculates your Chart, he or she must consider many factors in the time element. What time zone were you in at the time of birth? Was it Daylight Time or Standard Time? What Sign (by Degree) was at the zenith when you were born? In order to have your Chart figured correctly, it is necessary to calculate by sundial real time - that is when the Sun was directly over your city would be true noon time. It could be at 11:52 A.M. or 12:34 P.M., for instance. Before the railroads in the United States standardized time for their schedules in 1883, all Noon time was figured locally by whenever the Sun reached its zenith point. It was impossible to develop a train schedule with all those different times.

So the transcontinental train system was the impetus to establish uniform time zones in the United States. Alaska had four time zones until 1983 when the zones were cut to two. The Midheaven on your Chart is the true Zenith point in your locality at the moment of your birth.

## TIME AND TWINS

Many people ask about astrological comparisons of twins. The studies that I find the most interesting are the ones being done on twins who have been brought up separately. A recent study has been done at the University of Minnesota. Phil Donahue and other talk show hosts have interviewed twins who have been reunited as adults. The Similarities have been amazing. One show featured two young women who had been adopted separately at birth. They both worked as cosmetologists and both sang in their church choirs.

Several years ago, there was a great deal of press and TV coverage concerning triplets who had been separated at birth by adoption. They were never told that they were part of a multiple birth. All three young men lived on the East Coast. Triplet #1 started college and met someone who had known one of his brothers at the same school the previous year. When triplet #1 did not respond to the name of triplet #2, he was eventually shown a picture of #2 in the school yearbook. After the first two brothers were reunited, their picture was carried in many newspapers. Imagine the shock of triplet #3 when he saw the photograph and read the story! When all three were brought together, people were stunned by their similar qualities. All three smoked the same brand of cigarettes, they all participated in wrestling as their major sport, and all had been discipline problems in high school.

Jesse Stearn in his book A Time For Astrology researched what he termed "astral twins" — people born at the same time in the same city. He writes about two young men who were born in the same place and time. They went to the same college and joined the same fraternity. When they were 21 years of age, there was a fire in the fraternity house and both young men died in the fire.

# CONCEPTS

My approach to teaching astrology is by concept. I want students to think about the meaning of the Planets, Signs, Houses, and Aspects in their basic terms. So many people think they must know lengthy descriptions. I tell my classes that doctors and lawyers cannot memorize everything that goes on in their professions, but they do know how to find answers and descriptions in their reference books. That is how we should learn astrology. We must learn to understand the simplest meanings, and then know how and where to find good and thorough descriptions. My approach to this book is to take a vast and complex subject and whittle it down to the basics. The basics, along with all the visual aids, are helping my students make astrology a part of themselves much quicker than the methods I studied under in learning beginning astrology.

To try to bring the most important parts of astrology into concept form, I suggest you think of the 12 names of the Constellations as the A,B,C,'s of astrology. The A is Aries. The Zodiac always begins with Aries. The calendar year began in the spring when the Sun reached zero Degrees of Aries, from the time of the Julian Calendar in 45 B.C. until the Gregorian Calendar was adopted by England and the American Colonies in 1752. The New Year then began on January 1. The Gregorian Calendar balanced the time more evenly since our Earth's rotation is not exactly 24 hours. In a year's time, the Earth would be off by approximately twenty seconds from its rotation of the previous year. The Gregorian Calendar was developed under Pope Gregory XIII in 1582. It decreed that three days would be omitted each 400 years, so in 1700, 1800 and 1900 we did not have leap years, but in the year 2000 we will, to adjust for the build-up of time difference. It was not until 1752 that the Gregorian Calendar was adopted by English speaking countries. When this occurred, the new year began on January 1 instead of on the vernal equinox, which is zero Degrees of Aries.

# THE 1, 2, 3 's OF ASTROLOGY

Some beginning astrology students have difficulty understanding how Planets are placed on the Wheel. I tell them that they must learn to count astrologically. Instead of 10's, 20's, 30's, etc., we count from 0 to 29 Degrees of each Sign, starting with Aries:

| | | | | | | |
|---|---|---|---|---|---|---|
| 0° | Aries | 0° Taurus | 0° Gemini | 0° Cancer | 0° Leo | 0° Virgo |
| 1 | | | | | | |
| 2 | | | | | | |
| 3 | | | | | | |
| 4 | | | | | | |
| 5 | | 5 Taurus | 5 Gemini | 5 Cancer | 5 Leo | 5 Virgo |
| 6 | | | | | | |
| 7 | | | | | | |
| 8 | | | | | | |
| 9 | | | | | | |
| 10 | | 10 Taurus | 10 Gemini | 10 Cancer | 10 Leo | 10 Virgo |
| 11 | | | | | | |
| 12 | | | | | | |
| 13 | | | | | | |
| 14 | | | | | | |
| 15 | | 15 Taurus | 15 Gemini | 15 Cancer | 15 Leo | 15 Virgo |
| 16 | | | | | | |
| 17 | | | | | | |
| 18 | | | | | | |
| 19 | | | | | | |
| 20 | | 20 Taurus | 20 Gemini | 20 Cancer | 20 Leo | 20 Virgo |
| 21 | | | | | | |
| 22 | | | | | | |
| 23 | | | | | | |
| 24 | | | | | | |
| 25 | | 25 Taurus | 25 Gemini | 25 Cancer | 25 Leo | 25 Virgo |
| 26 | | | | | | |
| 27 | | | | | | |
| 28 | | | | | | |
| 29 | | 29 Taurus | 29 Gemini | 29 Cancer | 29 Leo | 29 Virgo |

and on through the next six Signs ending with 29 Degrees Pisces, and starting over again with zero Degrees Aries.

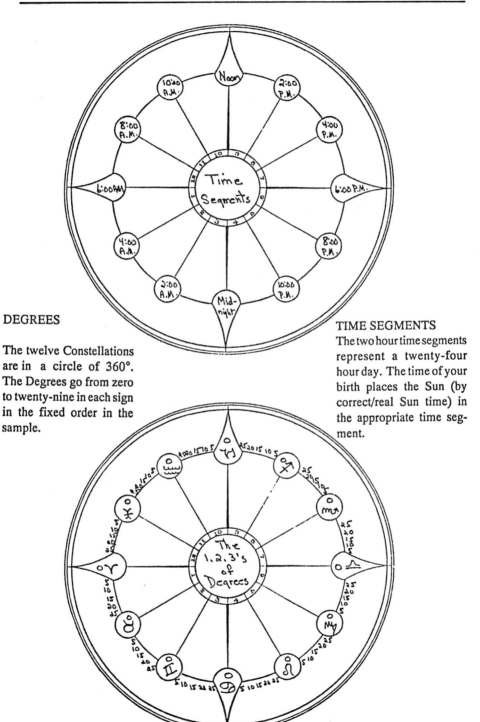

## DEGREES

The twelve Constellations are in a circle of 360°. The Degrees go from zero to twenty-nine in each sign in the fixed order in the sample.

## TIME SEGMENTS

The two hour time segments represent a twenty-four hour day. The time of your birth places the Sun (by correct/real Sun time) in the appropriate time segment.

# THE A, B, C's OF ASTROLOGY

Learning the sequence of the 12 Constellations is like learning the A,B,C's of a language. Our astronauts have had to learn the sequence and the various star groupings in each Sign. Until 1929, the divisions between the Constellations were irregular, like the dividing lines of the continental United States. In that year, however, world astronomers agreed upon a straight line division for the Constellations. The word Constellation is from the Latin "con" meaning "with" and "stella" meaning "stars."

I gradually learned the sequence of the Signs from memorizing my own Chart. But in hopes of aiding students of astrology, I have developed the following memory associations.

| SIGN | ALPHABET LETTER | MEMORY ASSOCIATION |
|---|---|---|
| Aries | A | For Aries with the arrival of Spring. |
| Taurus | B | For Bull, the symbol of Taurus. |
| Gemini | C | For Communicating, what Geminis do best. |
| Cancer | D | For Domestic. Cancer is the Sign of domesticity. |
| Leo | E | For Elegant. Leos have a touch of class and/or nobility. |
| Virgo | F | For Fortitude. Virgos can handle the lengthy, nitty-gritty details. |
| Libra | G | For Good at relating. Libras are the public relations people. |
| Scorpio | H | For Hidden. Scorpios like |

|  |  | secrets.  They like to probe hidden things. |
|---|---|---|
| Sagittarius | I | For Intellect. Sagittarius rules the 9th House of the higher mind. |
| Capricorn | J | For Journey.  Capricorns make a life-long journey climbing up the mountain of success. |
| Aquarius | K | For Kindness. Aquarians are the humanitarians of the Zodiac. |
| Pisces | L | For a Loving heart. Pisces is the last Sign and the most sympathetic. |

# LEARNING TIPS

1. Read and re-read this book as if you are studying a script. Underline key words. Underline important phrases. Put an asterisk in the margin whenever you think something is crucial.

2. Write important information in your own hand from the most significant pages. On an episode of the situation comedy "Growing Pains," the teenage son is flirting with a failing grade in history. To help pass a test, he writes important information on the bottom of his gym shoes. When he sees the test he says, "Hey, I know this stuff!" There is no better way to imprint the parts of astrology that you want to memorize than by writing notes in your own handwriting.

3. Read some every day.
   Immerse yourself a la "Berlitz Method." Read over important sections for 15 minutes in the morning and again just before bedtime.

4. Keep your Chart next to you as you study.
   Keep a diagram of the glyphs in front of you. Write the glyphs often — don't be afraid that they don't look as good as you'd like. It takes practice.

5. Find a friend who is interested in astrology so that you have someone to talk with about the subject. That way you can practice your speaking ability in this new language.

6. When using other astrology books, read the parts that interest you. Trying to read thick books from cover to cover sometimes discourages students. Read things relating to your Chart.

7. Textbooks
   As you get further into your study of astrology, you should have a good textbook. If I only owned one textbook, I would choose The Astrologer's Handbook by Frances

Sakoian and Louis Aker. If I owned three books I would add The Rising Sun - Your Astrological Mask by Jeanne Avery and Planets In Aspect by Robert Pelletier.

If you wish to own a second general textbook, Astrology, A Cosmic Science by Isabel Hickey is excellent. It is written from a spiritual view rather than a psychological or humanistic view. The Compendium of Astrology by Rose Lineman and Jan Popelka is a very fine encyclopedia of astrology.

There are many very good books on astrology. I think the best way to choose any other books is to search through the ones available at your library and book store. Our response to books is very personal. I like to be comfortable with the format as well as the text of a book.

# THE ASPECTS

When the 360 Degree circle of the Zodiac is divided by 1/4 or 1/2 or 1/3, certain tensions seem to be expressed between the Planet energies whose orbits are within those divisions. For instance, a right angle in geometry is a 90 degree angle. In astrology, this is called a Square Angle. When two Planets are 90 Degrees from each other in Celestial Longitude (within an orb of 7 Degrees), the energy represented astrologically is said to be difficult or discordant. If the Zodiac were divided by 1/4's it would form 90 degree angles. This is the hardest Planetary Aspect. It is also the most energized. It makes you work harder in the areas of life where the Square Planets sit by House Placement. The Square acts like a friction toy. You try and try, and then suddenly things move forward with momentum.

If the circle were divided by 1/2's, the Planets would be 180 degrees apart. This Aspect is called an Opposition. The Planet harmony would feel tension, as if you were being pulled in two directions simultaneously. While this can be a difficult Aspect, it is not as hard as a Square, since compromise is possible. The energy is more passive.

If the circle were divided by 1/3's, it would produce Aspects 120 degrees apart. This Aspect is called a Trine. It is an Ease Aspect, where the energy between the Planets flows harmoniously. The Trine indicates vitality and enthusiasm. For example, a Trine between the Sun and Mars would represent a smooth flow of physical energy, as well as harmonious ego energy. Mercury Trine Neptune would indicate a creative imagination. Trines usually bestow talent and ability. It seems to give you a flair in whatever quality is represented by the Planets.

When Planets are 60 degrees apart, the Aspect is called a Sextile. The Sextile is another favorable Aspect, but is not quite as strong as a Trine. It often indicates mental ability and brain power. It usually represents opportunities occurring in the areas of life where the Sextile makes contact in the Chart. The opportunities in the life of someone with many Sextiles in the Natal Chart often appear as luck to other people. Sextiles are a minor Aspect, and the orb involved is narrowed to 5 Degrees.

The other Minor Aspect is the Inconjunct. This Aspect occurs when two Planets are 150 Degrees apart. The orb is narrowed to less than 3 Degrees. This Aspect produces great inner tension.

One important factor to remember with Aspects is that they are colored by the Sign and House the Planets occupy. Also, the Planets involved in an Aspect could receive contact from other Planets at the same time, and this would alter the Planetary energy. The Natal Charts of prominent achievers have a mixture of Hard and Ease Aspects.

The most important Aspects are the ones involving contact with the Sun, Moon, Ascendant, or Midheaven. Contacts between the faster moving Planets (Sun, Moon, Mercury, Venus, Mars) to the slower moving Planets (Jupiter, Saturn, Uranus, Neptune, Pluto) are more significant than Aspects from one slow moving Planet to another. The Aspects that are involved in what is called a Configuration have tremendous importance.

A large number of Aspects is an indication of a very busy life and/or complex person. In some old astrology books, the Hard Aspects are described in very negative terms. Astrologer Don Jacobs has an excellent way of distinguishing between the Hard and Ease Aspects. (Ease means an easy or harmonious flow of energy.) He says, "Any Aspect of Venus and Mars, for instance, is going to make you sexy. The strength of the angle and your ability to handle the sexiness depends on the angle. The difference is not in kind, it's only more or less of the same thing."

| ASPECTS | GLYPH | ACTION | MEMORY ASSOCIATION | ANGLE |
|---|---|---|---|---|
| Conjunction | ♂ | Power Intense Assertive | The O with an arm extended to make a close connection | Within an orb of 7° |
| Sextile | ✳ | Ease Opportunities Often gives mental sharpness | Sharp angle - like a knife; acute angle in geometry | 60 degrees, 5° orb |
| Square | ▢ | Stress Difficulties Disharmony of Planetary energy | Hard edge of a table Right angle in geometry | 90 Degrees, 7°orb |
| Trine | △ | Great ease Ability Natural flow of Planetary energy. | The laid-back ease of a lounge chair. Obtuse angle in geometry. | 120 Degrees, 7° orb |
| Inconjunct | ⊼ | Great strain Disharmony by Element and Quality. | The line on top hides the angle of the inner stress. | 150 Degrees less than 3° orb |
| Opposition | ☍ | Tension Being pulled in two directions | Tug-o-war rope. Straight line angle. | 180 Degrees, 7° orb |

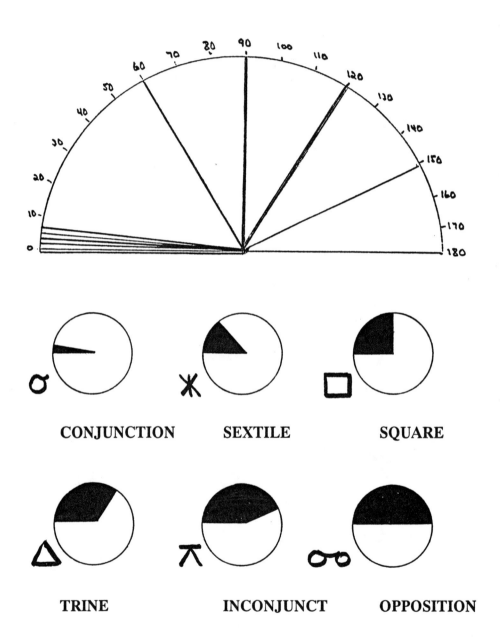

**A PLANET WITHOUT ANY ASPECTS IS WEAKENED**

# THE CONJUNCTION

The Conjunction occurs when two Planets are close to each other in Celestial Longitude. The Planets should be in an orb of seven Degrees or less. There are times when three or four Planets can be in this alignment at the same time, but that is infrequent. A Conjunction adds strength and power to the Chart. If you remember the childhood game of "Red Rover, Red Rover, I Dare You To Come Over," you can envision two people holding hands to block someone from crossing over into "their territory." They have much greater strength than someone "standing guard alone." The glyph "symbol" for the Conjunction is a circle holding out an arm. The Conjunction usually indicates talent in the area of the Chart where it occurs. The energy of the two or more Conjunct Planets blend together to form an intense and very strong Aspect. This is the most powerful Aspect.

# THE SEXTILE

The Sextile is an acute angle of 60 Degrees. Since it is a very sharp angle, it is easy to remember that it usually bestows mental sharpness. It also indicates opportunities in life that you have to be sharp to take advantage of. I've found many Sextiles in the individual Charts of celebrities who seem to be very lucky. One of my students, who graduated first in one of the Colleges of Engineering at a large University has a Chart with a tremendous number of Sextiles. She has a fabulous job. She says that she has almost been embarrassed by the wonderful number of opportunities and choices that she has had in life.

# THE SQUARE

The Square is a right angle in geometry, which is a 90 Degree angle. This is one of the hardest Aspects, as the Planets involved do not function together in harmony. There will be friction in life in the areas where the Square Planets fall by House location. A Square causes us to try things over and over again to get ahead. But like a friction toy, all that energy that we expend in trying will suddenly push us ahead. The people who achieve a great deal will usually have a combination of Hard and Ease Aspects. The Square produces action.

## THE TRINE

The Trine is an obtuse angle of 120 Degrees. It's an Ease Aspect. It's a comfortable energy like the laid-back ease of a lounge chair. The energy represented by the Planets involved flows in harmony like the stride of horses in harness. Trines indicate ability and talent. Isabel Hickey, in her marvelous book, <u>Astrology, A Cosmic Science</u>, describes Trines as virtues which have been achieved in the past. Too many Trines, without any Hard Aspects in the Chart, could incline a person to be an underachiever. It could make life too easy.

## THE INCONJUNCT

An Inconjunct is an Aspect of 150 Degrees. Some astrologers consider this to be the most difficult of all the Aspects. There is tremendous inner tension. There is no Sign compatibility by either Quality or Element. This is a Minor Aspect.

## THE OPPOSITION

The Opposition is a 180 Degrees Aspect. It occurs when two Planets are on opposite sides of the Chart. This is considered a Difficult Aspect, but not nearly as difficult as the Square or Inconjunct. An Opposition creates tension, and seems to pull you in two different directions simultaneously. This feeling of tension can keep you striving for balance. The reason that the Opposition is the least difficult of the Hard Aspects is because compromise is always possible. For example, if a woman has Moon Opposition Saturn in her Chart, she can be torn between caring for her family and home and wanting a career. A possible compromise would be a part-time job outside the home that would still leave her enough time for family responsibilities.

# SUMMARY

The Aspects give tremendous insight into what makes us tick. We see our assets and liabilities in black and white. The problem areas of our life can be seen in the Hard Aspects. Help for these problems can be found in any Ease Aspect contacting a Planet which is also involved in a Hard Aspect. We can concentrate on using the harmonious energy flow — accent the positive — and make our difficulties diminish.

# THE ASPECT CONFIGURATIONS

There are four major Configurations that can occur in a Natal Chart. A Configuration is when three or more Planets combine to form one of the following:

1.  The T Square
              When two Planets in Opposition are both in Square Aspect to a third Planet. The T Square gives the greatest energy possible. While the energy produced is intense, there is a release valve, when the energy is focused through the House opposite the focal point of the T. The focal point of the T produces a prominent Planet.

2.  The Grand Trine
              When two Planets in Trine Aspect to each other are both Trine a third Planet. This is the second most energizing Configuration that can be found in a Chart. It offers a powerful flow of harmonious energy. When both a T Square and a Grand Trine appear in the same Chart, it gives the Chart the greatest energy possible.

3. The Grand Cross

When two Oppositions are Square to each other, forming a Cross. This is the most difficult Configuration producing strong tension. The strength of the Grand Cross is at its strongest in Cardinal Signs. Since there is no release valve as in the T Square, the energy can be dissipated. The Grand Cross produces a very forceful, dynamic personality.

4. The Stellium

A Stellium occurs when three or more Planets are in the same Sign. This brings a strong influence of the Sign in the Chart interpretation. The House where the Stellium is located becomes more prominent.

## PLANETARY ASPECT DIFFERENCES IN TWO CLOSE CHARTS

The two Charts used for this demonstration belong to two women who are friends. They were born two days apart. It will give you an idea of how much the fast moving Planets change in such a short time. Since the Sun moves one Degree per day, their Suns are two Degrees apart. Chart I has her Sun at 12° of Sagittarius, while Chart II has her Sun at 14° of the same Sign. Chart I has the Moon in Gemini at 6°. Since this is an Air Sign, the emotional nature is much more detached than the Moon in Chart II where the Moon is at 7° of Cancer, — a very emotional Water Sign. The Moon has moved 31° in the two-day period. Mercury in Chart I is in Sagittarius at 27°. Mercury in this Sign produces a mind that is concerned with attitudes rather than facts. There is usually an interest in Ninth House matters. Thinking is often along acceptable, traditional lines. They have a knack for knowing what the public is going to like. This placement would be an asset in an advertising or writing career. Mercury here indicates very direct speech. It also gives acute perception. Chart II has Mercury at 1° of Capricorn. This indicates an in-depth mind, with mental discipline, strong powers of concentration, and organization. The mind is practical and often ambitious, since Capricorn is the Natural Ruler of the Tenth House of career. Venus and Mars have both moved only one Degree.

Both Charts still contain the major Configuration of a Grand Trine between the Sun, Mars and Uranus. Chart II has an additional Configuration due to the rapid movement of the Moon. This Chart has a T Square with the Moon Opposition Saturn Squaring Uranus in the First House. Since the Moon has moved into Cancer in this Chart, it has produced a Stellium with Jupiter and Pluto also in Cancer. The Cancer Stellium becomes very prominent in this Chart. So Chart I has one Configuration in her Chart, while Chart II has three Configurations.

While the two friends have many connecting points between their Charts, they have enjoyed spotting the differences. The difference that they get the biggest kick out of is in the Second House. Chart I has Capricorn on the Cusp, with Saturn in the House. She is very conservative with money — her husband almost has to force her to buy things. Chart II has Aries on the Cusp, with its Ruler Mars very active in the Chart. This woman likes to spend money as soon as she earns it!

## TWO CLOSE CHARTS:

Showing Differences in Aspect
Configurations Occurring
in Two Days Time

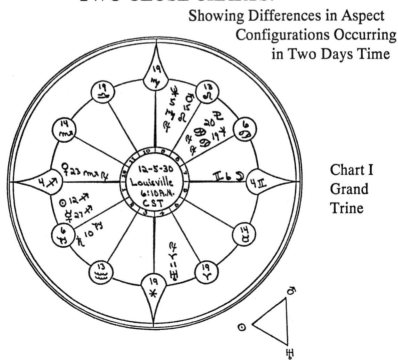

Chart I
Grand
Trine

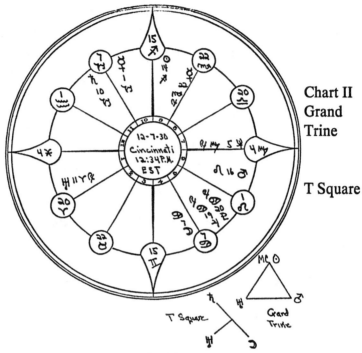

Chart II
Grand
Trine

T Square

Stellium: Moon, Jupiter and Pluto
in Cancer

# 3

## The Mechanics
## of the Chart
## Celestial Reasonings

# CELESTIAL REASONINGS

A problem that some new students have is understanding how the Solar System diagram fits on the astrological Wheel. With one class that was having a great deal of difficulty with this, I hit upon the idea of having a see-through plastic copy of a Chart made at a quick print store. I showed them an empty Chart form, then laid the clear plastic sheet showing the Planets on top. I could almost see the light bulbs go on in their heads!

# FIRST IMPRESSIONS: HEMISPHERE EMPHASIS AND CHART SHAPES

The first thing that I notice about a Chart is called the Chart Shape and Emphasis. This means what Shape is made by the groupings of the Planets and in what section of the Chart they are located.

# HEMISPHERE EMPHASIS

The Hemisphere Emphasis of a Chart means which section of the Chart contains the most Planets. There are two divisions: first, the Chart can be cut in half vertically by the Meridian. If most of the Planets fall on the right side (called the Eastern Hemisphere where the Sun rises), it indicates a person who can call his own shots in life. If most of the Planets fall on the left side (called the Western Hemisphere where the Sun sets), it usually means that this person's life will be greatly affected by circumstances and outside influences. The second division is when the Chart is cut in half horizontally by the Horizon. If most of the Planets fall in the upper half, the person is said to be more outgoing, objective and an early bloomer. If most of the Planets fall in the bottom half, it indicates a person who is more inward, subjective, and often a late bloomer. There can be more interest in spiritual matters rather than worldly matters.

Marc Edmund Jones, in his book entitled How to Learn Astrology, has an excellent section on the interpretation of Chart Emphasis.

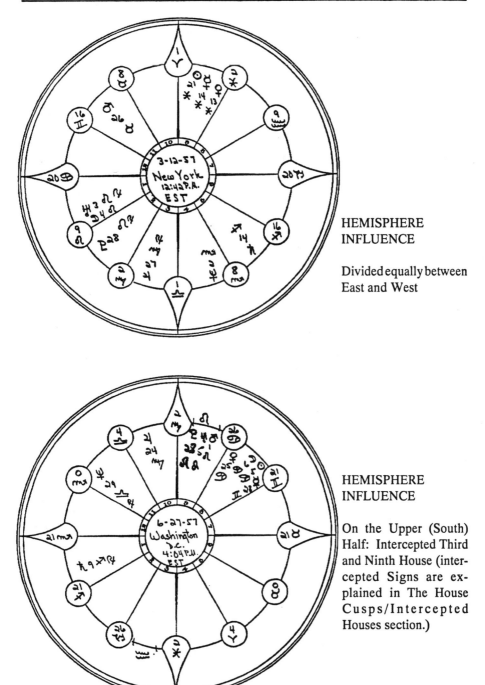

HEMISPHERE
INFLUENCE

Divided equally between
East and West

HEMISPHERE
INFLUENCE

On the Upper (South)
Half: Intercepted Third
and Ninth House (inter-
cepted Signs are ex-
plained in The House
Cusps/Intercepted
Houses section.)

# CHART SHAPES

The Chart names are simple descriptions of the Planet groupings. Not all Charts will fit into a Chart Shape perfectly, but there will usually be one which each Chart most closely resembles, or the Chart might have a variation combining two Shapes.

# BUNDLE

A Bundle occurs when all the Planets are bunched together — just visualize a bundle of logs for example. This indicates narrowed interests with great focus on the matters of the few adjacent Houses where the Planets are located. Many of the great geniuses in history have had Bundle Charts. When Conjunctions occur within the Bundle, it adds great power to the Chart. All the Planets should fall within 120 Degrees. The Chart can indicate a narrowness of opportunities.

# LOCOMOTIVE

To form a Locomotive, all of the Planets should fall within the space of two Trines — 240 Degrees. Like a locomotive wheel, which it resembles, this Shape gives strong self-driving power to the Chart. The Lead Planet (clockwise) going into this open area is important.

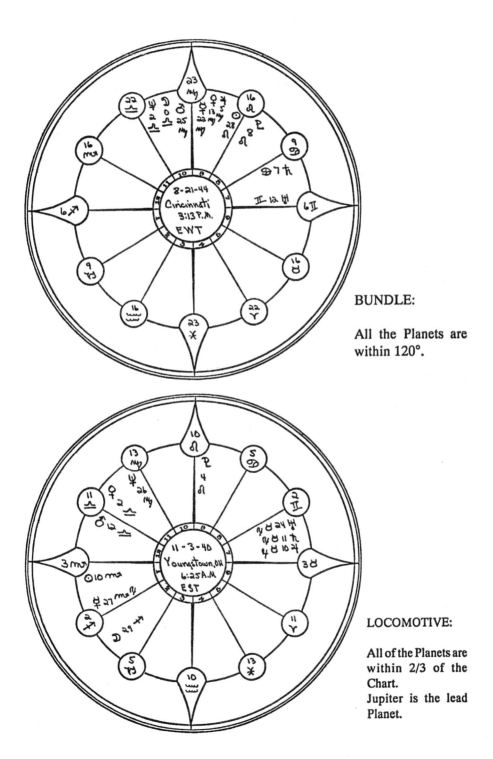

BUNDLE:

All the Planets are within 120°.

LOCOMOTIVE:

All of the Planets are within 2/3 of the Chart.
Jupiter is the lead Planet.

## BOWL

A Bowl Shape means that all the Planets fall within one-half or 180 Degrees of the Chart.  If you think of a Bowl as a container, it will help you remember that people with this Chart are self contained.  Activity in life comes from the half of the Chart where the Planets lie.  The Lead Planet, that is the last Planet before the open space going clockwise, becomes important, with all the other Planets pushing their energy through the Lead Planet.

## BUCKET

The Bucket looks like a Bowl with a Handle.  The Handle usually has one Planet in it, but it can be a Conjunction of Planets.  As in the Bowl, the Lead Planet has emphasis, but the most important Planet is the one found in the Handle.  All the other Planets should pour their energy through the Handle.  This is significant in career planning, as you can gain insight by which Planet is in the Handle, as well as the placement by Sign and House.

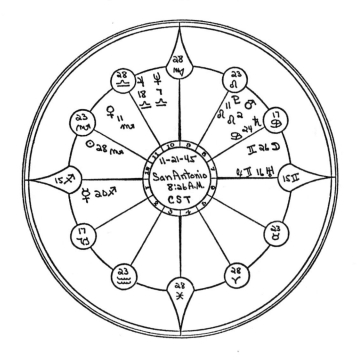

**BOWL CHART:**

All Planets are contained within 180°. The Lead Planet in this Chart is Uranus (7th House). All the Planets, except Mercury, are above the Horizon.

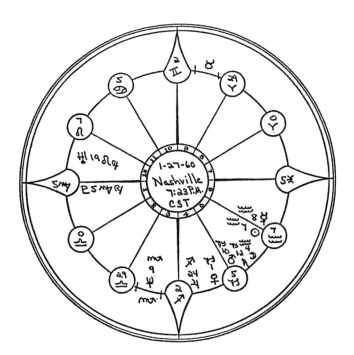

**INVERTED BOWL:**

All the Planets are below the Horizon except Uranus, in this Bowl Chart. Intercepted Third and Ninth House.

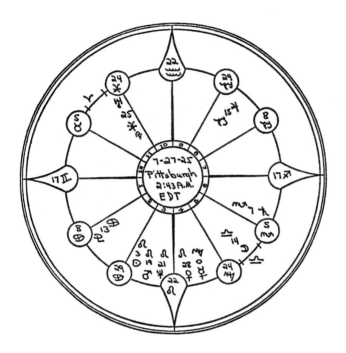

**BUCKET:**

Uranus is the focal Planet in the Handle of the Bucket (11th House). Pluto is the Lead Planet (2nd House). All the Planets, except the Handle Planet, are within 180°

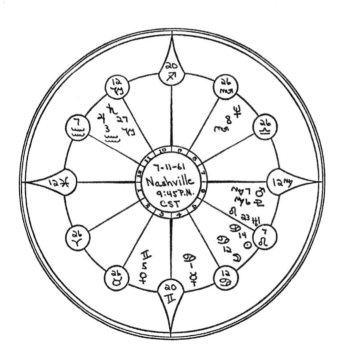

**BUCKET:**

Two-Planet Handle: Jupiter and Saturn are the Conjunct Planets in the Handle (11th House). Venus is the Lead Planet (3rd House). This is similar to the Bucket, with this one exception.

## SLING

The Sling is a little similar to a Bowl, but think of a slingshot in trying to visualize its Shape. Like a slingshot, it can have concentrated power.

## SPLAY

The Shape of the Splay looks like the spokes of a wheel. When the spokes are fairly evenly spaced, it represents a self-directed individual. When the spokes are not evenly spaced, there is usually less stability.

## SPLASH

The Splash is easy to spot as it has the most Houses filled. Since there are twelve Houses and only ten Planets, all the Houses cannot contain a Planet. At least seven Houses should have a Planet. This Chart indicates a person with a wide variety of interests.

## SEESAW

A Seesaw pattern occurs when the Planets are clustered on opposite sides of the Chart. This Shape usually contains several Oppositions. People with this Chart are able to see both sides of a problem.

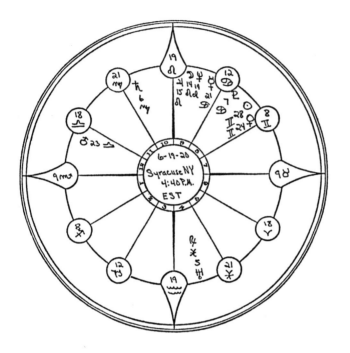

**SLING:**

Similar to a Bucket, but all the Planets (except the Handle Planet) are within the 120° instead of the 180° of the Bucket Shape.

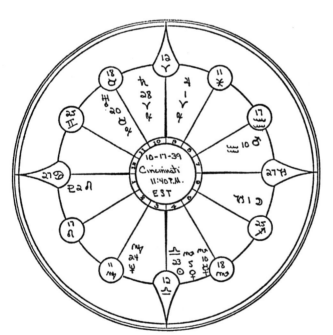

**SPLAY:**

The shape of the splay looks like the spokes of a wheel. When the spokes are fairly evenly spaced, it represents a self-directed individual. When the spokes are not evenly spaced, there is usually less stability.

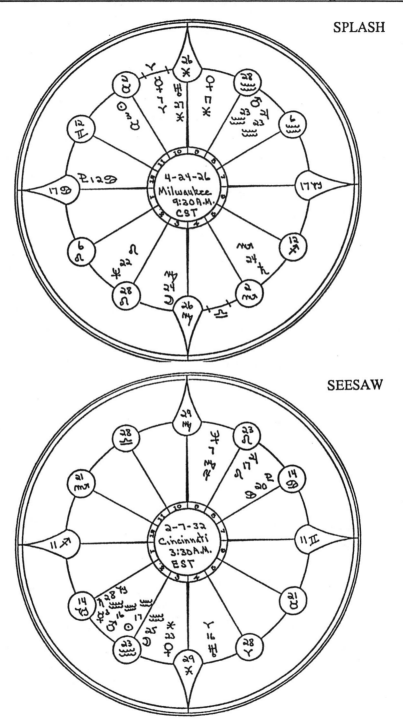

# THE CHART CROSS

The Chart Cross is made up of the four major points that form the Axis of the Chart — the Ascendant, the Midheaven, Descendant, and Imum Coeli. The Latin words, Imum Coeli, abbreviated I C represent the midnight point on the Chart and is opposite the Midheaven which is the Noon point. The Ascendant is at the 6:00 A.M. Sunrise point opposite the Descendant which is at the 6:00 P.M. Sunset point. The Midheaven is designated on Charts by the initials M C which stand for the Latin words Medium Coeli, which means middle of the heavens. The Imum Coeli means the bottom of the heavens.

Unless a Chart has intercepted Houses, the Cross will either be a Cardinal, Fixed, or Mutable Cross. Since the Axis is so important, the type of Cross gives an instant clue in understanding the drive of the individual. The Cardinal Cross is the most dynamic; a Fixed Cross means great perseverance, and a stubborn resistance to change; and a Mutable Cross indicates a very flexible person.

# RELATIONSHIPS OF PLANETS, SIGNS AND HOUSES

On the natural Zodiac Wheel, which begins with Aries on the First House Cusp, there is a relationship between the Planets, Signs and Houses. Aries is the "me first" Sign, so it relates naturally with the First House of the self. So wherever Aries is on your Chart, you want to be first at what you do in that House. Mars, the Ruler of Aries, is your ego energy, so it relates to the self no matter in which House it falls.

Taurus relates to possessions and values. Its Ruler, Venus, is the Planet of possessions. You will like beautiful possessions related to the matters of that House. You will also love things represented by that House. Where Taurus sits on a House Cusp is where you can be possessive toward that area of life. You will want that part of your life to have beauty in it because of the Rulership of Venus.

So, if you try to think of the concept of the relationship between the Planets, Signs and Houses, it will help you to interpret a Chart. Wherever Cancer falls on a House Cusp you will want to nurture that area.

# AN EXAMPLE OF CHART CROSS INFLUENCE

The Axis of the Chart, also called the Chart Cross, can produce a dynamic personality when the four points are in Cardinal Signs. The sample Chart belongs to an extremely dynamic man. He is the #1 regional sales manager of a large national company. He has the Power Planet, Pluto, in the Tenth House of career. Before I put his Chart into my computer, I guessed that he had a prominent Mars, and possibly a strong Aries contact. He has Mars in the Ninth House Conjunct the Midheaven, which is a strong Aspect. But I think the terrific dynamic energy that people see in him comes from his Cardinal Cross. He has all the Cardinal Signs in the same zero Degree on his Axis!

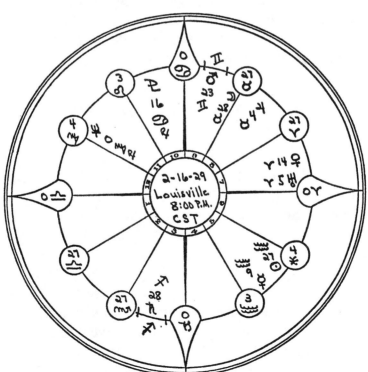

# DECANS

The thirty Degrees of each Sun Sign are divided into three sections of ten days, called Decans or Decanates in astrology. The Decans give a fine tuning to the Sun Sign descriptions. The first Decan of a Sign covers the first ten days of a Sign. This Decan is the most pronounced in the characteristics of the Sun Sign Ruler. For instance, the first Decan of Aries would show a very strong Mars influence (Mars is the natural Ruler of Aries). The second Decan (the next ten days) would have characteristics of the Ruler of the next Sign by similar Element — in this case the next Fire Sign is Leo so the Sun would help shade the Aries personality. The third Decan (the third ten day segment) would include the influence of the Ruler of the following Fire Sign, Sagittarius. So the third Decan people would be colored by a Jupiter connection. While this seems confusing to some students, it proves very interesting and accurate when you read the descriptions of the Decans in textbooks. Astrologer Marguerite Carter has some very good work on the Decans in her book, The Time When Your Luck Will Change: According To Your Birthday. This book can be found among the reference books in the education department of some public libraries. The Compendium of Astrology, by Lineman and Popelka, has a good section on Decans also.

# THE DEGREES ON THE CUSPS

In teaching students how to think of House Cusps, I suggest that they think of the Sign on the Cusp as the name of a street. For instance, I grew up on a street named Observatory Road. My address there was 2822. So, I say that the address is like the Degree on the Cusp. And the Sign of the Zodiac on the House Cusp is similar to the street name of that House. If the Degree on the Cusp is 22, that is like the address. Therefore, 22° Taurus, for instance, on the Second House Cusp, is like 2822 Observatory. So, if you had to place a Planet on the Wheel: for example, if Venus were at 18° of Taurus in this Chart, you would place it in the First House. The Signs, as well as the Houses, are running in a counter clockwise manner, so any Degree of Taurus before 22 would belong in the

First House. If Mars were at 26° of Taurus, it should be placed in the Second House.

# DEGREES AND MINUTES

While I don't put the Minutes on the Natal Charts of beginning students because is confuses most of them, I do explain how their Charts will look after they get used to reading the Degrees. On computerized Charts, the Planet Glyph is placed first on the outer circle of the Wheel, followed by the Degree, the Sign and then the Minutes. In Celestial Longitude, there are sixty Minutes in each Degree. So, if Venus at 18 Taurus had 32 Minutes after it, the Degree would still be 18. But, if the Minutes became sixty, that would change the Degree to 19. Where the Minutes must be understood is when a Planet falls in the same Degree as a House Cusp. If a Fifth House Cusp were at seven Degrees, seventeen Minutes of Cancer, and the Moon were at seven Degrees, nineteen minutes of Cancer, the Moon would be placed in the Fifth House. If the Moon were at seven Degrees, fourteen Minutes, it would be in the Fourth House.

# EMPTY HOUSES

Some people are thrown by "Empty Houses" in a Chart. They ask, "What does that mean? Won't I have any activity in that area of life?" At this point, I explain that all twelve Signs of the Zodiac are affecting our Chart. (This is discussed at the beginning of the chapter on interpretation.) Initially, I just teach that the Sign on the House Cusp describes the way we approach the activity of that House. For example, wherever Aries is, we approach the matters of that House with energy, enthusiasm and courage. So, apply a few key words of each Sign to the Houses. As we progress in the beginning course, I introduce Planetary Rulers. They are the key to understanding the activity of Empty Houses. How Mars, the Ruler of Aries, is Aspected will tell you a lot about how you handle your

Aries House and so forth. The Houses occupied by Planets are usually the most active areas of a person's life.

## WHEN THERE ARE PLANETS IN A HOUSE

Once students understand Empty House Rulers, the next question that arises is who is the "boss" when there are Planets in a House? Is it the Ruler of the Sign on the House Cusp or the Planet in the House? If it's Taurus on a House Cusp, Venus the Ruler of Taurus, "owns" that House. Now let's say that Venus owns that House, but Jupiter "lives" there. Which one is more important? Just think in real life — if you rent a house, does that home reflect you or the owner? The answer is you. That house holds your furniture, your accessories, your hobbies, your plants, your pets, your family and friends, your entertainment, etc. So, you have the most impact on the House, even though it is still owned by the person holding the deed. So, Jupiter would have more strength in a House, even if Venus rules the House Cusp. This is the same for any House containing any Planet or Planets.

While the Planet in the House has more influence than the Planet ruling the House, both Planets do affect the activities of the House. Some astrologers think of the Ruling Planet of the House as a co-ruler with the Planet in the House. In other words, there are a chairman and a co-chairman.

## THE HOUSE CUSPS

Many students wonder about the Degree numbers on the House Cusps. First of all, whatever Degree number is on the First House must also be on the Seventh House in the opposite Sign. This is true for all the Cusps. If you know the first six House Cusps by the Degree and Sign, you could fill in the last six House Cusps. When studying the Constellations, you learn that the same Signs are always opposite each other, and that the order of the Signs is constant.

Next, there is a problem understanding the different Degrees on some of the House Cusps. We have to keep several factors in mind. First, our view of the Solar System is from Earth. The axis of the Earth is tilted, so our view is from an inclined angle. Then the path that the Earth follows around the Sun is not a circle, but an ecliptic path, which further distorts our view. The farther away from the equator, the more angled the view becomes. One of my beginning classes had a great deal of trouble visualizing this distortion, especially when it caused Intercepted Houses. If you are able to visualize perspective in painting, it will help you picture the view of the Constellations from Earth.

## INTERCEPTED HOUSES

An Intercepted House means that a Sign falls completely inside a House without appearing on the Cusp. The opposite Sign must also be intercepted. The farther north or south you were born from the equator, the greater the possibility for Interceptions. To try to explain why the view is distorted, I use the two major sports arenas that are adjacent on the Ohio River in Cincinnati. The Riverfront Stadium is used for the Cincinnati Reds baseball games and the Bengals football games. It is a perfect circle. If you stood in the center of it, you could see all the seats in the stadium in exactly the same width. The Coliseum, which is used for basketball games, concerts and ice shows, has an elliptical shape. If you stood in the middle, the seats at the ends and in the middle could be seen in the same width, but the seats in the corners would be visually "pushed together" and appear narrower. So, Intercepted Charts are the results of the perspective view from Earth. The Signs that are Intercepted in a Chart are less visible in the psychological makeup of the individual. The energy of the Intercepted Sign is slow to develop.

## INTERCEPTED PLANETS

When a Planet is located in a Sign that is Intercepted in a House, it functions in a similar manner as does the Intercepted Sign. The Planet will not be prominent in the Chart. The energy represented by the Planet will be self-contained and not apparent to other people. If the Intercepted Planet is a fast moving one (Sun, Moon, Mercury, Venus, or Mars) the energy can eventually grow out of the Interception as the person matures. This growth can be indicated by the Progression of the Chart. Progressions are explained in the chapter on Rectification.

# THE NODES OF THE MOON

The Nodes of the Moon, also called Lunar Nodes, are not Planets, but rather the points where the orbit of the Moon intersects the elliptic path of the Earth's orbit. The point of contact when the Moon touches the Earth's orbit moving north toward the north celestial pole is call the North Node. (The glyph for it looks like ear muffs, so I use the association with the north being cold to help students remember which Node is which). The South Node is the point of contact on the elliptic moving toward the south. (The glyph is an inverted symbol of the North Node). It is very confusing to many new students to see the glyph for the Moon's Nodes on their Charts. So during the first course, I delete the Nodes from the Charts. I add the Nodes to the class Charts after the first eight weeks. All of the celebrity Charts in this book will show the North Node. The South Node is not shown, but is always directly opposite the North Node.

The traditional view of the Nodes is that the North Node has a Jupiter effect, in that it's thought to be a beneficial point. The South Node has a Saturn effect as it's supposed to indicate a point of restriction. The Nodes become significant when they are involved by Aspect with other Planets. The Nodes are believed by many astrologers to give karmic information in the Chart. Where the North Node is located, you should try to achieve. Where the South Node is placed indicates old habits that should be released.

# RETROGRADES

Eight of the Planets have apparent Retrograde motion at times during the year. The eight are Mercury, Venus, Jupiter, Saturn, Uranus, Neptune and Pluto. Retrograde means that at certain times during the year these Planets can appear to be moving backwards by Celestial Longitude. This is only by appearance, as all Planets continue to move always in forward motion. It happens when a faster moving Planet passes a slower moving Planet. When you are riding in a car, bus, or train, you can witness this Retrograde effect. As you pass a slower moving vehicle, it appears to be moving backward, even though it is still moving forward. The symbol for Retrogrades is like the $R_x$ on a prescription.

When Retrograde motion occurs, the Planet energy slows down. If you have Retrograde Planets in your Natal Chart, the energy will be more internalized and will develop slowly. Many astrologers believe that Retrogrades add strength to the Chart. There are many famous, highly intelligent people with Mercury Retrograde in their Natal Charts. Their mental processes are unusual in that they do not think the way most people do. Mercury goes Retrograde three times a year for about three weeks each time. This is the one Retrograde that is very apparent in our daily living. When you hear newscasters or talk show hosts flub their lines, it's almost always during a Mercury Retrograde transit. During these periods when Johnny Carson's words won't come out right, he laughs and asks if the Moon is full. He's close, in that it is caused by Planetary motion. The most important thing to avoid during Retrograde Mercury transits is the signing of contracts. Something can easily escape your attention.

# THE RELATIONSHIP OF THE SIGNS TO THE HUMAN BODY

From ancient times, astrology has related the Zodiac Signs with the human body. The connection begins with Aries and the head, down through Pisces and the feet. The principle of correspondence apparently dates back to the days of the pharaohs. It was believed that there was a medical relationship between the Signs and the body, with the Signs on the Sixth and Twelfth Houses giving indications of health problems. The Sign on the Sixth House could indicate minor health problems. The Sign on the Twelfth could show the problem area that might cause hospitalization. The Ascendant, which represents the physical self, can also show a medical problem relation by Sign.

Hippocrates, the famous Greek physician (460-377 B.C. approximately) who was the first doctor to insist on scientific study of disease, required the study of astrology by his students. He believed that astrology showed possible predisposition to different diseases. Astrology teaches that the ailments are not inevitable, but only possibilities.

The correspondence is as follows:

| The Sign | The Parts of the Body | Possible Ailments |
|---|---|---|
| Aries | Head, face | Headaches, congested sinuses, eyestrain |
| Taurus | Neck, throat | Sore throats, stiff necks, larynx and vocal chord problems |
| Gemini | Arms, shoulders, lungs, nerves | Lung problems, bursitis, arthritis |
| Cancer | Stomach, breasts, general metabolism | Susceptible to disease, colds, alcoholism |
| Leo | Heart, spine, lower back | Heart problems, lower back  pain |
| Virgo | Abdomen, digestive tract | Intestinal upsets, elimination problems, allergies, worry |
| Libra | Kidneys, adrenal glands | Kidney stones, diabetes, cystitis |
| Scorpio | Sexual organs/reproductive system; bladder | Susceptible to infections in these areas; strong recuperative power |
| Sagittarius | Hips, thighs, liver | Fractures of the hips or femur bones, sciatica |
| Capricorn | Knees, bones, teeth, skin | Chronic disease, colds, skin problems, anxiety |
| Aquarius | Ankles, calves, circulation | Varicose veins and hardening of the arteries; accident-prone, especially involving the ankles |
| Pisces | Feet, lymphatic system and the glands | Low vitality, water retention, drug sensitivity and/or problems |

# Interpretation
# How to put it all together

The lines of a plaintive song ask:
"Why was I born?  Why am I living?
What do I get?  What am I giving?"

The answers can be found in your Natal Chart.  The Signs on the House Cusps give a lot of information.  The Planets in the Houses give more direction and the interaction between the Planets "make your engine run."

The Signs on the House Cusps bring the characteristics of the Sign to that particular area of life.  For instance, wherever Aries is on the Cusp of a House, we put energy and drive into the activities of that House.  We can be courageous.

Where Taurus is, we can have great strength and perseverance.  We can also feel possessive toward the matters of that House.  There can be an Element of beauty since Taurus is ruled by Venus.

Where Gemini is on the House Cusp, we like a lot activity.  If it is on the Fourth House Cusp, we might want to own a second home, such as a vacation home, or we might want our home to have lots of activities with an accent on intellectual affairs.  When Gemini is on the Tenth House Cusp, we might work at two different careers simultaneously — the dual influence of Gemini should be felt in the House wherever Gemini sits.

With Cancer on the Cusp, there is an emotional attachment and a tenacity with the House matters.  We want to nurture in this area.  There can be changes and fluctuations because of Cancer's Ruling Planet, the Moon.

Wherever Leo falls on the House Cusp, we want to be creative in that part of our life.  We can bring a dramatic energy to the activities of the House.  We enjoy being in the spotlight.

Virgo on a House Cusp indicates the area of life where we will pay great attention to details.  We can be critical here, but we serve willingly.

Balance is the element we bring to the House where Libra sits on the Cusp.  If Libra is on our Eighth House Cusp, we will help balance our partner's income and we like to relate about Eighth House matters.  If it's on the Eleventh, we will serve as a balancing agent between friends, and relate well with them.

Where Scorpio sits, we are not content with surface matters, we will probe to the depths and meanings of the matters of the House.

Luck enters the House where Sagittarius falls on the Cusp since

Jupiter is the Ruling Planet. People with Sagittarius on the Second House Cusp are usually very lucky at making money. Sagittarius likes new challenges so we can feel restless if we can't keep growing, expanding, or going on to something new. With Sagittarius on the Tenth House Cusp, we can have several completely different careers in a lifetime. Once we conquer a career, we want to search out and conquer another. We can also work at two different jobs simultaneously.

We will apply steady energy to climb to the top wherever Capricorn is on the House Cusp. We usually have good managerial ability in the matters of the House and it often shows a business connection for us. If Capricorn is on the Eleventh House Cusp, we will probably serve as chairman, or president of different groups and organizations.

Aquarius brings an interest in new and unusual things within the matters of the House. We can have an intellectual approach to the matters of this House.

Where Pisces occurs on the House Cusp, there will be great sensitivity toward the activities of that House. We can be very imaginative here as well as intuitive. We can also have a spiritual approach to the House matters.

## PROCEDURES FOR INTERPRETATION

There are many different ways to study a Chart. I'm listing the method that is most comfortable for me.

1. The Placement of the Sun is the most important point in the Chart. It shows by Sign and House what the individual is striving to become or achieve in this life. Examine Aspects to the Sun, especially Conjunctions. Look at the House with Leo on the Cusp.

2. The second thing to examine is the Moon by Sign in order to understand the emotions, and the emotional attachment by House location of the Moon. Study the Aspects to the Moon, especially Conjunctions. Note the Placement of Cancer on a House Cusp.

3. The next most important consideration is the Ascendant. Study the descriptions of the Sign which appears there. As you begin to learn the Ruling Planets of each Sign, you will see that the location of the Ruling Planet of your Ascendant colors and modifies your Ascendant. The Ruling Planet of your Ascendant is called the personal Ruler of your Chart. Any Conjunction to the Ascendant is very important, or to its opposite point, the 7th House Cusp/Descendant.

4. The Midheaven is the next most significant point. Any Conjunctions to it are extremely important, or to its opposite point, the 4th House Cusp/IC. Other aspects to the MC should be studied.

5. The Planets
    By Sign.
    By House location — First House Planets are very important.
    By Element.
    By Quality
    Stelliums (if any) — Stelliums are very significant because of their strength.

6. Aspects
    The Aspects are the internal working parts of your engine. They have tremendous significance in the understanding of your Chart. I suggest that you use a fine text book like Planets In Aspect by Robert Pelletier and study your Aspects in detail. Also, note the strength of the Aspects — the tighter the orb, the stronger the influence. If the Aspect is applying (coming toward an exact orb) it is stronger than a separating Aspect (when the Planets have already passed exact orb).

7. Power Indicators
    The number of Planets in Angular Houses (the 1st, 4th, 7th and 10th).
    The number of Planets in Cardinal Signs.
    The conjunctions involving Personal Planets with Ascendant,

Midheaven, or slow-moving Planets.

The Power Planet -

The Planet in a Chart with the greatest strengths -— the strength can come from multiple Aspects to the Planet; the Planet can be part of a Configuration, or it can be part of two different Configurations. It could be in an Angular House, especially the First House. It could be a focal Planet.

8. Chart Shape - Is it a Bowl, Bucket, Bundle, Locomotive, See Saw, Sling, Splash or Splay?

9. Hemisphere Emphasis - Do the majority of the Planets lie in the top half — the Southern Hemisphere — or the bottom half — the Northern Hemisphere? Are more Planets on the left side — the East? — or the right side — the West?

First House Planets have tremendous importance in the Chart. They strongly influence the personality and the physical body. Brief examples of what the Planets would indicate in the First House:

Sun       -   Great vitality/love to shine in the spotlight

Moon      -   Very emotional personality with fluctuating moods

Mercury   -   Makes the person extremely mental (very active mind)

Venus     -   Usually bestows good looks/can make the person feel good about himself or herself (self love)

Mars      -   Gives tremendous energy/always likes to be on the go

Jupiter   -   Gives a buoyant, optimistic personality/can favor life's circumstances

Saturn    -   These people are born old and seem to get younger as they age. Very responsible and reliable. Early achiever.

loved in childhood, and in giving love. Susceptible to depression.

Uranus     -    Since Uranus lets you use your ingenuity wherever it falls in your Chart, when it's in the First House it makes you very ingenious. You'll march to your own drummer throughout life. You can be an original with Uranus here.

Neptune    -    In the First House, Neptune makes you very sensitive to drugs and alcohol. Half the dosage of most medications is often enough. It can also give you a strong spiritual influence. There can be an elusive quality in the personality. Often indicates artistic and/or musical talent.

Pluto      -    Placed here, Pluto adds great power to the personality. It gives an intense, probing disposition making the person want to deal with things on a deep, serious level.

One of the helpful things that I urge students to do is to take one of their Planets — for instance, Mercury, and write out the most prominent characteristics of your Mercury by Sign and House Placement. I suggest that they use a good textbook, plus another book they like that gives good descriptions of each Planet by Sign and House. I then recommend that they write phrases from the books describing each Aspect that is made to their Mercury. It really drives the information home. It's amazing how this can teach you to fully understand your abilities.

Another way that you can gain some interesting insight from your Chart is by reading the meanings of all your different Planet Aspects. Planets In Aspect by Robert Pelletier is an excellent book for this. As you read the Aspects, make a note of each career ability mentioned. For instance, Mercury Trine Pluto bestows talent in crime detection, medicine, research, engineering, pathology and surgery, according to Pelletier. As you read on, if a particular career is mentioned a second, third, or fourth time, mark it as such. You should see a pattern emerge with several talents showing the strongest. This can be a wonderful source of guidance in career choices. It's also interesting and fun.

# INTERPRETATION OUTLINE
## For Quick Reference

This is only a suggested method for reading a Chart. I have listed the most important parts of the Chart to study first.

1.  Sun: Sign and House
    Moon: Sign and House
    Ascendant: Ruler of Ascendant by Sign and House
2.  Aspects: To the Sun, Ascendant, Moon, Midheaven first; then
        to the Descendant and IC; to the other Planets
3.  Chart Shapes
4.  Elements
5.  Qualities: Expression or blending
6.  Houses: Angular, Succedent, Cadent
7.  The Personal Planets
        After the Sun and Moon:
        Mercury
        Venus
        Mars
    Use Planet meaning combined with key words of the Sign
8.  Stelliums
9.  Configurations:
        Grand Trine
        T Square
        Grand Cross
10. Prominent Planets:
        Heavily Aspected            First House
        Cardinal Signs              Lead Planet in Chart
        Angular Houses              Part of a Configuration
        Conjunction to:             Focal point of T Square
        Sun, Ascendant,             or Bucket-Shaped
        or Midheaven                Chart

As I teach my students how to begin to interpret Charts, I like to use the Charts of famous people. It's much easier to relate the characteristics of someone well known to a class. It's been fun to do these Charts and see repeated House emphasis among people in the same profession. For instance, many prominent actors and actresses have Planets placed in the First House of personality, the Second House of talent and ability for making money, and the Fifth House of creativity. In Doris Chase Doan's book, Astrology, 30 Years Research, there is some interesting information on the Charts of 100 movie stars. Of the 100 Charts analyzed, 91% had active First Houses, and 93% had active Fifth Houses. The most prominent Planets were Mars in 98% of the Charts, Uranus in 94%, Neptune in 89%, Mercury in 79%, and Venus in 74%. Doris noted that the strong Mars was necessary for the long hours involved in moviemaking. Uranus well Aspected indicates a magnetic personality with talent for originality and ingenuity. The stars with Neptune prominent were able to play a wide range of roles and not just one type. Mercury's importance would be in quick-wittedness, which aids in acting and staying power. The influence of Venus would be seen in beauty, grace and style.

The Charts used in this chapter are just the briefest samples of Chart interpretation. I'm pointing out a few characteristics that stand out prominently in each Chart. When you have your Chart fully interpreted by an astrologer, it takes about one and a half hours. The detailed computerized Charts run between 30 to 35 pages.

Whenever I prepare a Chart for interpretation, I write a breakdown of all the Aspects by symbol. Most Chart forms show the Aspects in graph form, similar to a mileage chart in a road atlas. I have developed my own system of listing the Aspects. I find my method seems to make the Aspects jump off the page for me. You will see this system with one celebrity Chart.

I also do a breakdown of Planets by Elements and Qualities. An ideal Chart would have a balance of all the Elements and Qualities. Doris Hebel, in her book, Chart Interpretation, has a wonderful section on when an Element or Quality is missing in a Chart. She suggests for physical well-being that if you're missing an Element (meaning there is only one Planet, or none, in a particular Element) you should try to surround yourself with whatever Element is missing. She thinks this will make you happier, and I agree. She says if you're missing Fire, try to live somewhere with a fireplace. If that's not possible, use candles on your table. If there is no Air, you should try to live where fresh air can always be circulating, and listening to music should be beneficial. If there is no Water, have a fish bowl or an aquarium, or float a flower in a bowl of water (if you do this, the water should be changed every 2 1/2 to 3 days because the Moon rules Water and changes Signs that often.) When there is no Earth in your Chart, put lots of live plants in your home.

When the Elements and Qualities are grouped for a Chart, we look at which Element and which Quality dominate by having the most Planets. Then we blend this Element and Quality to find how that person "expresses" from that standpoint. This just gives us more information in trying to understand the whole person.

There is a further refinement on the Houses used in interpretation. The Houses located on the Chart Cross or Angles, the First, Fourth, Seventh, and Tenth are called Angular Houses. Angular Houses have the greatest strength, with the strongest being the First House, followed by the Tenth House, the Seventh House, and the Fourth. The next grouping of the Houses is called Succedent, and those Houses follow the Angular Houses in counterclockwise fashion, as the Houses are numbered. The Succedent Houses are the Second, Fifth, Eighth, and Eleventh. Planets placed in Succedent Houses are not as strong as those placed in Angular Houses. The third grouping is the weakest. This grouping is called Cadent. The Cadent Houses are the Third, Sixth, Ninth, and Twelfth. When I interpret Charts, I do a breakdown by Houses to show additional strength of the Planets.

For those readers who would like a more advanced book on interpretation, I recommend Complete Horoscope Interpretation by the outstanding San Diego based astrologer, Maritha Pottenger.

# ASTROLOGICAL SIGNS WITH PLANETARY RULERS

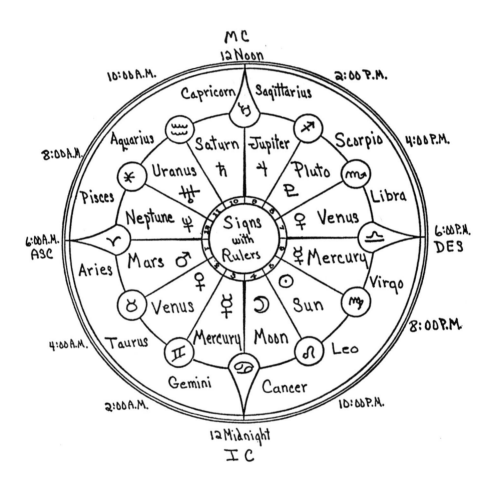

# Celebrity
# Charts

# JOHNNY CARSON

Johnny Carson's Chart has a Splash Shape which shows in the wide variety of his interests. One of his greatest assets is his genuine interest in the vast and changing array of guests he interviews. With Sun and Mars in the Twelfth House and a Scorpio Ascendant, no wonder people are always asking "What's Johnny Carson really like?" His communication skills are apparent with Mercury in his First House Conjunct the Ascendant and Conjunct Saturn. His Mercury (often described as your microphone in astrology) is beautifully Aspected. Besides the Conjunctions, Mercury is Trine Pluto and Sextile both the Moon and Jupiter. The Moon and Jupiter are Conjunct and located in his Third House of communication! So, his good fortune as well as his emotional comfort and security will be in Third House matters .

Venus in Sagittarius in the Second House of self-earned income is a lucky Placement. With Leo on the Midheaven, the public sees him as a classy guy. But with Uranus in the Fifth House of creativity, he dares to do some outrageous, but ingenious, comedy material. This Fifth House Uranus also indicates that he can be suddenly and strongly attracted in love situations. He has a Grand Trine and a T Square, with Pluto being involved in both major Configurations. This makes Pluto, located in the Ninth House of the higher mind, a very important Planet in his Chart.

With the Sun and Mars in the Twelfth House of behind the scenes, and Mercury in Scorpio (the Sign that likes secrets), there is an indicator of his interest and performance in magic tricks. Neptune in his Tenth House adds to his glamorous public image.

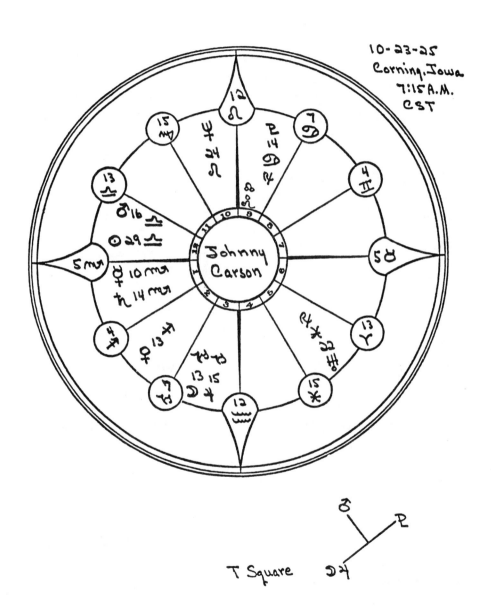

10-23-25
Corning, Iowa
7:15 A.M.
CST

Johnny Carson

T Square

# MARY TYLER MOORE

Mary Tyler Moore's Chart is a wonderful example of the actor's Signs being placed prominently on the House Cusps. She has Pisces on the Ascendant which gives her a very feminine, appealing look and a sensitive, intuitive personality. Sagittarius is on the Midheaven, another actor's Sign. Her Sun, which is in Capricorn, is in the Eleventh House (groups, friends, wishes) which greatly enhances her popularity. And it is Conjunct Jupiter, which is located in her Tenth House of career. She also has Mercury in the Eleventh. With Mercury and the Sun in that House, many people would like to have Mary as their friend. Another acting Sign is on her Fifth House Cusp of creativity. Cancer here with the Moon Conjunct Pluto in that Sign indicates powerful, deep emotions. The Cancer Moon adds more sensitivity to Mary's already very sensitive Pisces personality.

Mary's Venus is in the Twelfth House of "behind the scenes matters." I have found that many good actors and actresses will have a Twelfth House Venus or Sun showing a love of being behind the mask of someone else. Her Sun Trine Uranus gives her very magnetic appeal. Her many Sextiles add to her success, especially the Sun Conjunction of Jupiter, Sextile the Ascendant, and Venus Sextile the Midheaven.

There are two T Squares in the Chart adding a lot of power and drive. Her First House Planet, Saturn, shows a very responsible person. Saturn in the First House usually indicates people who are "born old" and seem to get younger as they age. They are very serious people who usually develop a sense of fun in their mid-thirties. Shirley Temple has Saturn in her First House making her very responsible as a child. With Neptune in the Seventh House, Mary seeks the ideal in marriage. Because of this idealism, she would not abandon a marriage easily. Neptune here also indicates a possibility of disillusion with the marriage partner. The Moon Opposition Mercury shows tension between her reasoning and her emotions.

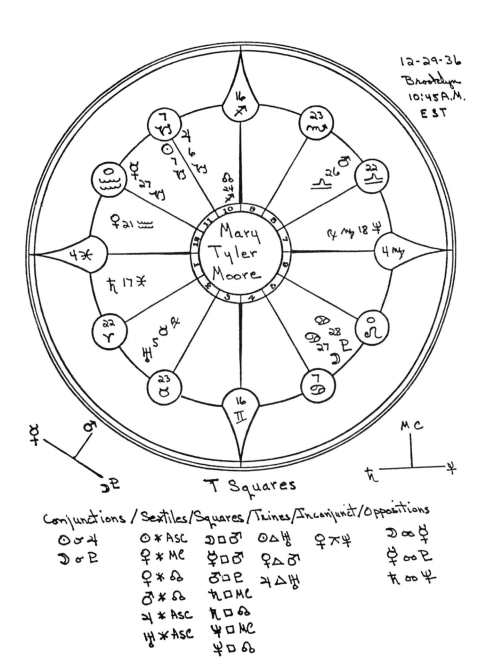

# BRUCE SPRINGSTEEN

Bruce Springsteen is an original. This is evident in his Chart by the Placement of Uranus in the First House. The Sun in Libra Trine Uranus makes him dynamic and also high-strung. Uranus is also Trine Venus adding to his magnetic, attractive appeal.

He has a loaded Fifth House (of creativity), with the Moon Conjunct Mercury, and Mercury Conjunct Neptune. This gives him powerful ability to combine his emotional nature (Moon), his mental ability (Mercury), and his imagination (Neptune). Venus is also in the Fifth giving him a love of creativity.

What type of singer will he be? We have to look at his Third House of communication to find the answer. With Leo on the Cusp, his style of communicating will be dramatic. With Mars in Leo in the Third, it will be very energized. With Pluto Conjunct Mars, his talent here will be tremendously powerful.

The Shape of his Chart is a Bucket that is almost a Sling Shape. He has Jupiter as the focal Handle Planet in the Eighth House which deals with sexuality. This would be one of the reasons many women find him so sexually attractive. The Lead Planet is Uranus giving additional importance to this already important Planet in his Chart. Six of his Planets are in Cardinal Signs, making him even more dynamic. He has one major Configuration in his Chart. He has a Grand Trine from his Moon to his Ascendant and Midheaven, giving him marvelous talent to express his emotions, and making this talent attractive to the public.

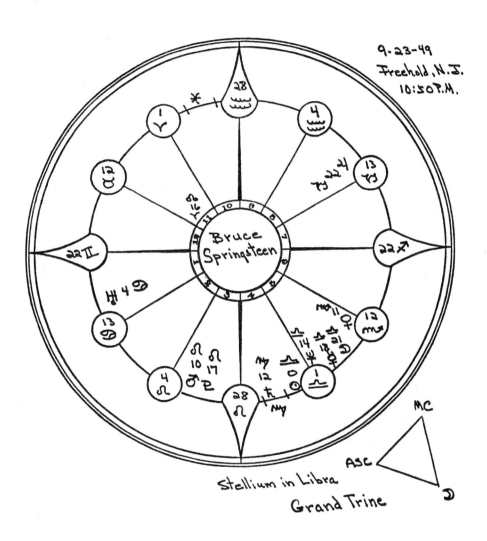

9-23-49
Freehold, N.J.
10:50 P.M.

Bruce Springsteen

Stellium in Libra
Grand Trine

MC
ASC
☽

# LENA HORNE

Since I've always thought that Lena Horne has the most sensually beautiful face that I have ever seen, I must admit that I looked at her Eighth House first. I wasn't disappointed. There sat Scorpio (the sexiest Sign) on her Eighth House Cusp. But what was even more exciting was to see the Moon in Scorpio just inside the Cusp. So Lena's emotional nature would be in the most powerfully intense Sign. Her Moon is beautifully Aspected to Venus in a Trine. Her powerful emotional nature would enable her to really "feel" the lyrics she sings. The Moon is also Square Uranus in the Eleventh House. Uranus here makes you original and attracted to unusual, creative people. It also makes you independent. Her Sun is Conjunct Pluto in Cancer. Since Cancer is another Water Sign, she would be even more deep feeling, intuitive, and emotional.

This Conjunction is Square her Ascendant giving her the push to succeed in a very competitive business. She has a lucky Sextile with Jupiter Sextile Venus, Saturn, and Neptune. Neptune and Saturn are in her Fifth House (of creativity). Jupiter is in her Second House (of self-earned income) giving her good fortune in that area. Mars is also there, so she puts her energy in this House.

With a singer, I always look at the Third House of Communication. Lena has Gemini on the Third House Cusp. Gemini is the most youthful Sign, so she should maintain the quality of her voice for a long time. Lena is blessed with a Stellium in Gemini. Mercury (your microphone) is in the Third House in Gemini — a natural Placement for it. Pluto is also in the Third House. What a wonderful place to have your Power Planet when you are a singer!

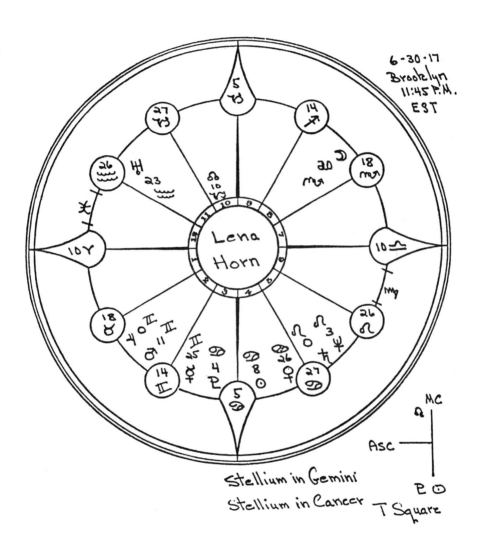

6-30-17
Brooklyn
11:45 P.M.
EST

Lena
Horn

Stellium in Gemini
Stellium in Cancer     T Square

# JOHN McENROE

John McEnroe was born in Weisbaden, Germany while his father was stationed there. I have long wanted to see his Chart. He is the most exciting tennis player that I have had the pleasure of seeing in tournament play. You can almost see the energy and tension jump out of his body. I wanted to see the Aspects in his Chart which would show his quick wrists and temper, as well as his fantastic physical coordination and talent.

Mars, which represents his physical energy, is in the Sign of Gemini (the same Sign placement for Mars in Pete Rose's Chart). This is a very quick dual Sign that likes to do two things almost simultaneously. It is in the Ninth House which indicates interest in outdoor sports. Mars is Trine the Ascendant which bestows great endurance and good physical strength. It indicates a very active person with a harmonious flow of energy.

The Sun is in Aquarius in the Fifth House — the area of fun and games. This is a terrific placement for an athlete. The Sun is Conjunct Mercury, and this Conjunction is part of a Grand Cross, which causes a tremendous amount of stress. John's Chart is overloaded with difficult Aspects affecting his temper. With Sun Square Mars he is easily frustrated and angered. This Square tends to give an assertive push to arguments. He is quickly irritated. The Square of Mercury to Jupiter tends to make the person opinionated, thoughtless, and there can be a lack of common sense. Mercury Square Mars causes restlessness, irritability, excitability, and a quick response to argue. The Moon Square Pluto makes a person irritable. And Mars Square Pluto makes him hot tempered as well as impulsive.

Any one of these Squares would be difficult. Just imagine how hard it would be to learn to handle John's three "double whammies!" Controlling his temper is much more difficult for him than for the vast majority of people. His Trines and Sextiles help relieve the pressure from all the Squares. The Moon Trine the Ascendant indicates a harmonious domestic life, and a good imagination. With Neptune Trine the Midheaven, there would be a good intuitive relationship with his parents. This Aspect shows talent in the arts, as actor, musician, or artist. With the Moon Sextile Uranus he could be unconventional in his romantic attachments (his out-of-wedlock child with Tatum O'Neal has been highly publicized — marriage followed.) This Sextile also gives magnetism, a good imagination and bestows versatility.  John shows these qualities in his TV commercials.

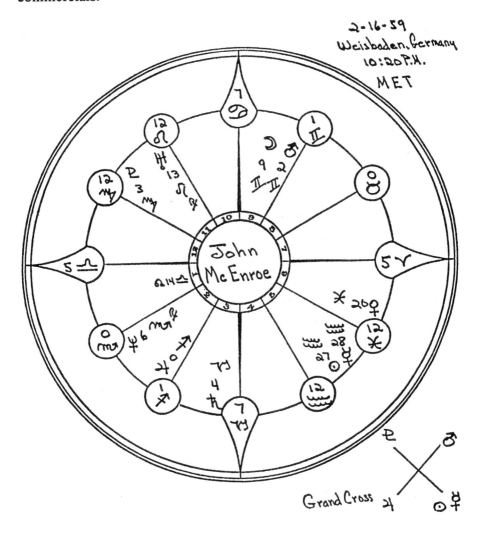

# MARILYN MONROE

Marilyn Monroe's Chart forms a Bucket Shape with Saturn in the Fourth House as the important Handle Planet. The Moon in the Seventh House is the Lead Planet, thereby having great importance, along with Saturn, in her Chart. She has the actor's Signs of Leo on the Ascendant and Sagittarius on the Fifth House of creativity. Her Sun is in Gemini Conjunct Mercury in the Tenth House of career and public image. So, she wanted to shine in the public's eye and she gave her mental energy to her career.

Neptune in her First House is a very significant placement. People with Neptune here, when it is afflicted, seem to have trouble focusing their aim in life. It also makes you extremely sensitive to drugs and alcohol. This is also true when Pisces, the Sign which Neptune rules, is on the Ascendant. Since Neptune is the Planet of the imagination, people with a First House Neptune are often very creative.

With Venus Conjunct the Midheaven, Marilyn would be very attractive to the public. Venus is Trine her First House Neptune. Her sex goddess image can be seen in her Eighth House which deals with sexuality. There she has Mars, the active energy for sex, in the graceful and appealing Sign of Pisces. Mars is Trine Saturn. It is also Inconjunct Neptune, giving her some stress and confusion in this area. The magnetic Planet Uranus, which is important in actors' Charts, is also in the Eighth House.

Saturn in the Fourth House often indicates problems with the father. When it is Retrograde also, as Marilyn's is, it usually indicates more trouble, often a father who isn't there in some way. The Moon, which has a secondary representation of your mother, is part of a T Square Opposing Neptune and Squaring Saturn. There would be confusion between her emotions and her imagination because of the Moon's Opposition to Neptune. With the Conjunction of the Moon and Jupiter, Marilyn's emotions would be greatly expanded.

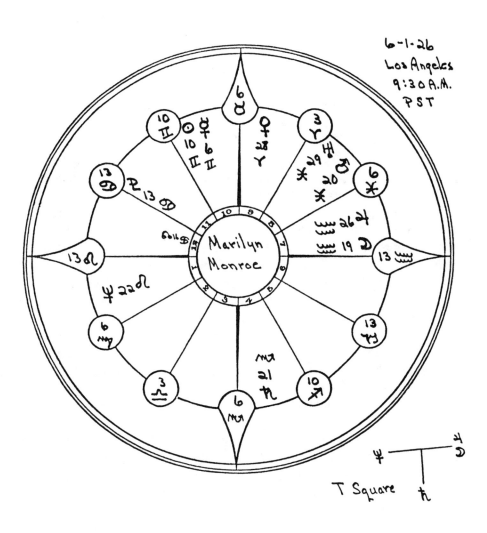

6-1-26
Los Angeles
9:30 A.M.
PST

T Square

# MADONNA

While there are similarities between Madonna and Marilyn Monroe, the differences are more striking.   While Marilyn was naturally sensual and vulnerable, Madonna's sexuality is manufactured, and she's one smart business woman. She is deliberately provocative and outrageous — always with an eye on financial success and publicity.

Madonna's birth time is listed as 7:00 A.M.  It gives her a Virgo Ascendant, which is usually an indication of shyness.  But it has three powerful Conjunctions to it with the Moon, Mercury, and Pluto (the Power Planet).  All these Planets are in the hard working Sign of Virgo.

The Eighth House represents sexuality.  Her Eighth House is ruled by Mars with Aries on the Cusp.  One of the representations of Mars is the sex act. Uranus represents the unusual and the unconventional.  Her Mars is Square her Uranus. So, Madonna likes to shock us with her attitudes toward sex. Mars also rules the Ninth House of religion.  So her approach to religion will also have a shock value.  Neptune is a spiritual Planet.  In Madonna's Chart, Neptune is Inconjunct the Midheaven.  So there is great strain with her public image and spirituality.  Venus (which deals with beauty and sensuality) is Square Jupiter (the Planet of expansion) and Neptune (the Planet of the imagination), so her sensuality will be at odds with beauty, leaving nothing to the imagination. It will be hard driving instead of graceful.

With eight Planets on the Eastern Hemisphere (left side of the Chart) she has great potential to call her own shots in life.  Barbara Streisand is another woman with many Planets on the left side of the Chart.  Both women are extremely capable of managing their own big careers.  Opportunity for self-earned income is indicated by the Second House.  Madonna has Libra on the Cusp which is ruled by Venus, indicating beauty as a factor in producing income. The Planet of expansion and good fortune, Jupiter, is luckily located in this House. Venus is located in her Eleventh House — the House of popularity and the financial payoff House of the career.  So the two Benefics (meaning beneficial), Venus and Jupiter, are very fortunately placed in her Chart. Her luck is enforced with the Sun Sextile Jupiter.

Another success indicator in her Chart is the Sun Square Mars, giving her a strong drive for success. It also makes her combative and reckless — I think she uses this Element in her performances. This Square also indicates a lack of restraint.

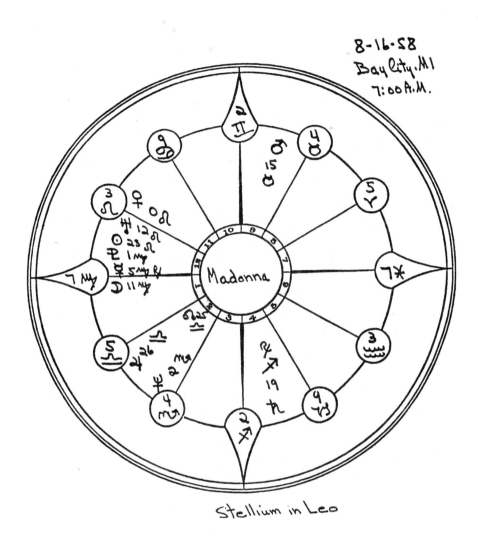

8-16-58
Bay City. MI
7:00 A.M.

Madonna

Stellium in Leo

# PETE ROSE

Pete Rose has a Bowl Chart with seven Planets beneath the horizon making him subjective. Eight of the Planets are on the Eastern, or left side, which has enabled him to call most of the shots in his life. His Aries Sun in the First House is a terrific placement, by Sign and House, for an athlete. His First House Mercury Conjunct the Sun gives him a quick mind. So Pete is what I would call a smart athlete. He uses his head, thinks and acts quickly, which has been a key to his great success as a hitter and base runner.

In an athlete's Chart, the next thing I look for is the Placement of Mars. Pete has Mars Conjunct Jupiter giving him a powerful and fortunate energy flow. The Planets are in Gemini, the Sign that likes to do two things almost simultaneously — again adding quickness to his physical energy.

The Fifth House is the House of fun and games which includes sports. Pete has the Power Planet Pluto in that House. Besides these prominent Planets, Pete has two T Squares in his Chart. He has a total of seven Squares giving him tremendous drive. The Fifth House is also the House of speculation, which includes gambling. The Ruler of his Fifth House is the Moon, which is part of his T Square. His Moon is Square Mars and Jupiter, which means his emotions are in conflict with his ego energy, and his good fortune. His Fifth House Planet Pluto (representing power) is Inconjunct Venus (representing money) in an Aspect of great tension. Both the Moon and Venus are in the Twelfth House of behind-the-scenes activity. Since Pluto indicates where we will experience regeneration, by House location, there can be reform of Pete's gambling habits.

The five Sextiles have added lucky opportunities in his life. The most outstanding Sextile is the one between the Sun and the Mars-Jupiter Conjunction. Sagittarius on the Midheaven is indicative of working in two different careers at the same time, and changes in careers. Pete was a player/manager, and now does some sports broadcasting.

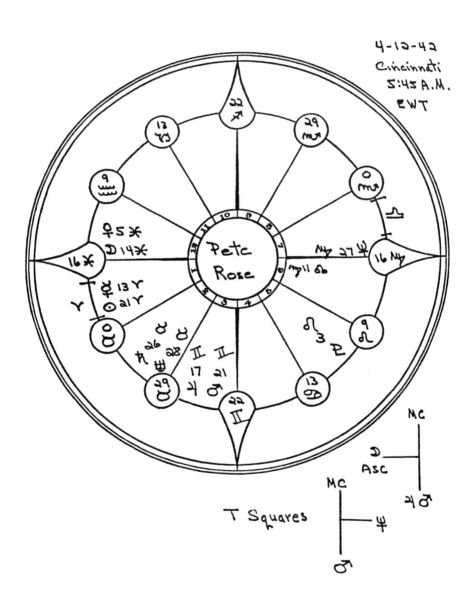

4-12-42
Cincinnati
5:45 A.M.
EWT

Pete Rose

T Squares

# JACKIE KENNEDY ONASSIS

The nobility of the Leo Sun is very apparent in Jackie Kennedy's Chart. She has Sun, Mercury, and Midheaven in Leo. She has a very regal bearing and a manner that says, "I'm here to be waited on." Her royal attitude served her well in keeping up appearances in spite of JFK's hyper sexual activity with an endless list of other women. Her own sexuality is very cool and detached with her Venus in the Air Sign of Gemini. Venus is in opposition to Saturn indicating the possibility of marriage to an older person and/or for money rather than love.

Besides the elegant side of her persona, the other outstanding characteristics are her desire to be mysterious and the fascination of the public toward her. The Scorpio Ascendant explains her desire for privacy and her secretive personality. Neptune (the glamour Planet) Conjunct the Midheaven (representing the public image) gives her the glamorous public mystique.

With Sun and Mercury in the Ninth House, she has an interest in foreign travel and people. Mercury here usually gives a facility with foreign languages. The Ninth House also represents publishing, so her career in publishing should be fulfilling for her.

The type of partner she needs is indicated by the Seventh House. With Taurus there, she seeks a solid, practical man with good money making ability. With Jupiter (good fortune) in the Seventh, she will be very lucky in partnership. The Eighth House is the area of your partner's money. With Venus (which represents money) and Pluto (power) in this House, she would be fortunate with her partner's finances, and money would influence her choice of a spouse. Since there is a Gemini influence in her Seventh House, there is an indication of two marriages — because Gemini is a dual Sign.

The Moon in Aries in her Fifth House is an interesting placement. When John Kennedy was killed, her fierce emotional nature wanted to fight as Moon in Aries would. Eight hours after the President died, Jackie was still wearing her blood-stained suit as if it were an embattled uniform. Her Moon is Square Pluto which can make her "one tough cookie." She has no Water Planets in her Chart. A woman with a strong emotional water influence in her Chart would not be able to bear to see her slain husband's dried blood on her clothing for that length of time.

The Shape of Jackie's Chart is a Bucket with Saturn as the handle Planet in the Second House. All the Charts I've seen with Saturn here indicate either a problem with having enough money or thinking you have enough. The Second House shows the talent we have for self-earned income. Saturn here does not inhibit talent, but does make self-earned money slow in coming.

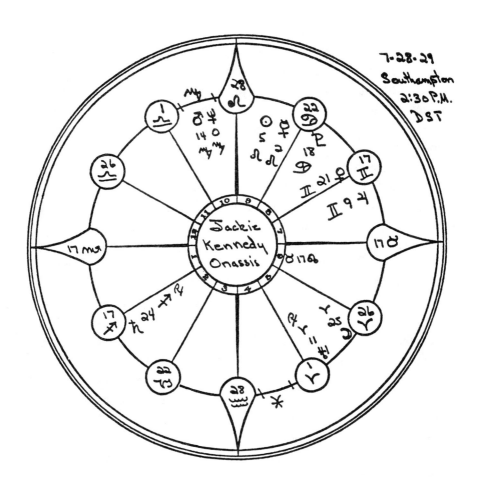

# HOWARD COSELL

Howard Cosell has been a sports broadcaster for many years. His greatest successes were in co-anchoring Monday Night Football and in boxing commentary. He has just published a book on sports. Howard Cosell's Chart contains many Aspects indicating a complex person. He has a T Square and a Grand Trine. Mars is involved in both Configurations. His very strong Mars is Square Jupiter, Neptune, and the Ascendant. The Mars Square Jupiter would make him excitable (the hyper energy type) with a quick temper. It would indicate an ego problem. He would tend to be controversial and power hungry. With Mars opposite the Midheaven, he's ready to take on the public in a fight. The Grand Trine of Venus, Mars, and Pluto intensifies his energy and his affections. The Trine of Mars to Pluto bestows self-confidence. It also gives him an adventuresome spirit with an enjoyment of a good fight.

His T Square tends toward unpopularity personally and with the public. Jupiter Square the Midheaven indicates a lack of humility and contributes to his grandiose manner.

The Sun in Aries makes Cosell a fiery, adventuresome, assertive person. Placed in the Ninth House, it aids his mental expression. The Moon in Gemini produces the incessant talker. It also makes him quick and versatile in his self-expression. The Moon in the Eleventh House is a popularity Placement, making social contacts very easy which has benefitted his career. His Sun is Trine Jupiter which gives great vitality. It usually bestows good judgment and a sense of responsibility. The Sun is also Trine Neptune which gives him a strong imagination. The Conjunction of these two Planets, Jupiter and Neptune, with the Ascendant, gives him a tremendously vivid imagination. The Conjunction is even more powerful as it pulls his Ascendant into the Trine with his Sun.

Since his career is in communications, I next look at his Third House. There are no Planets there, so we must look at Venus, the Ruling Planet of the Sign on the Third House Cusp. Venus is Conjunct Uranus, giving him ingenuity and creativity in communication. Venus is in an exact Trine with Mars, giving a harmonious energy low to his communicating ability. This Trine is also involved with Pluto forming a Grand Trine. Pluto adds great power. So his Third House ruler is beautifully

Aspected. With all this talent going for him, Cosell is still a controversial figure. Many people love to talk about how much they dislike him. Besides his T Square giving him antagonistic personal qualities, he has one other major difficult Aspect in the Sun Square Pluto. This Square indicates an ambitious power drive. It tends to make a person a braggart. It inclines to a dogmatic, quarrelsome personality. However, with Mercury in the Eighth House, Cosell is a good investigative reporter who digs down to the truth.

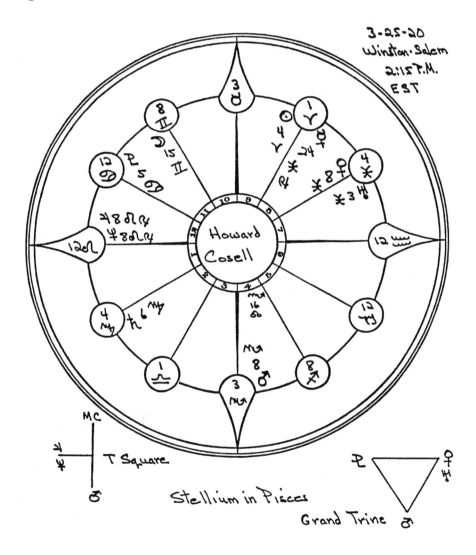

# JANE AUSTEN

Jane Austen was born in England in 1775. She was the first woman novelist to gain great fame. Her Sun is in Sagittarius in the Fourth House of the home. She wrote from her home. With Mars Conjunct Pluto in the Fourth House also, there is the indication of great power and energy aiding her in her life's work.

Neptune, the Planet of the imagination, is very prominently placed in her First House, in very close Conjunction with her Ascendant. This Conjunction is powerful in itself, but it is even stronger because Neptune and the Ascendant are Trine her Mars/Pluto Conjunction. Her First House is further enhanced by the Placement of her Moon in Libra there. This position gives an emotional balance to the personality. The Moon is Conjunct Saturn giving her self-discipline. This Conjunction is Trine Jupiter and her Midheaven, aiding her successful career.

With all but two of her Planets below the horizon, Jane was a subjective person who liked to know about the psychological makeup of people. The shape of her Chart is almost a Sling, with Jupiter and Uranus in a widespread Handle. The lead Planet is Neptune. This adds additional emphasis to her imagination. Many of the greatest English novelists thought that Jane had an unsurpassed skill in writing conversational repartee. With Mercury in Sagittarius in the Third House, her feel for conversation was intuitive, and light-hearted.

Her Seventh House Cusp is at 23 degrees of Pisces — a point of sorrow. No one could write better courting dialogue between a man and a woman, but Jane Austen never married. She died at age 41.

Her outstanding reputation as a novelist can be seen in her Chart with the placement of Jupiter (good fortune) and Uranus (originality) in the Ninth House of publishing. With the Conjunction of Jupiter to the Midheaven, she would have powerfully good luck with her career. These two Planets alone did not make her a writer, but in combination with her other Aspects, they contributed greatly to her success. Since the drive for success is seen in the Hard Aspects, I must mention that her Squares include Sun Square Neptune, Moon Square Mars, Mars Square Saturn, Saturn Square Pluto, Neptune Square the Midheaven, and finally the Sun Square the Ascendant.

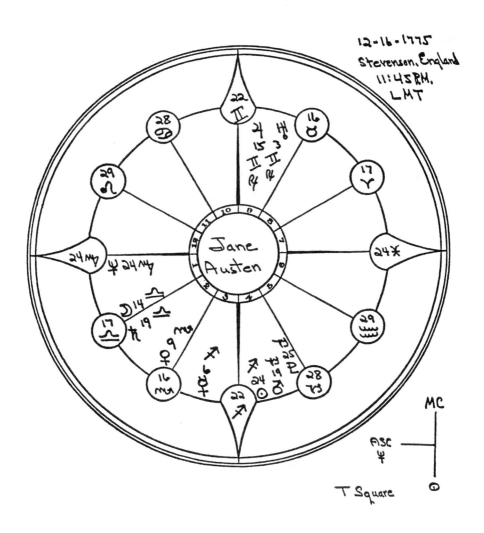

12-16-1775
Stevenson, England
11:45 P.M.
LMT

Jane
Austen

MC

ASC —
⊕

T Square   ☉

The Planet in highest ascension (the Planet closest to the Midheaven in clockwise motion ascending toward noon) in Diana's Chart is Neptune. Neptune is one of the two beauty Planets. It is also the glamour Planet since it rules the film industry. People with prominent Neptunes are usually very attractive to the public. (Jackie Kennedy Onassis has Neptune Conjunct the Midheaven). Diana's Sun is Trine Neptune. The Sign on her Midheaven is Libra. Libra is ruled by the other Planet dealing with beauty which is Venus. Libra is also one of the two most popular Signs. Adding strength to her Midheaven prominence is the Moon Trine the Midheaven. More power is added to this point by the Sextile of Uranus to the Midheaven. A prominent Uranus is a significant indicator of success with the public, as mentioned in the material quoted from Doris Chase Doan.

Two very significant Aspects are the Sun Sextile Pluto which gives her a healthy ego and great vitality, and Mars Conjunct Pluto, which gives her great self confidence, and intense physical and sexual energy.

Problems in relationships could develop through her T Square with Moon opposite Uranus, both squaring Venus. The opposition makes her very independent. Venus Square Uranus often shows sudden romantic attraction which can be of short duration. Venus in the Fifth House means love of children, a nice Placement which influenced her career before marriage to Prince Charles, and benefits her children.

With her Sun in the Seventh House, she'll shine her light the brightest in her partnership role. Mercury is also there. With a loaded Eighth House, she'll benefit from her partner's money. And with Moon and Jupiter in the Second House, she'll get comfort from her vast array of possessions.

Diana's Chart is a significant indicator of the public's fascination with her. There's glamour, charm, and strength galore. Her First House Planet Saturn will aid her in fulfilling her duties.

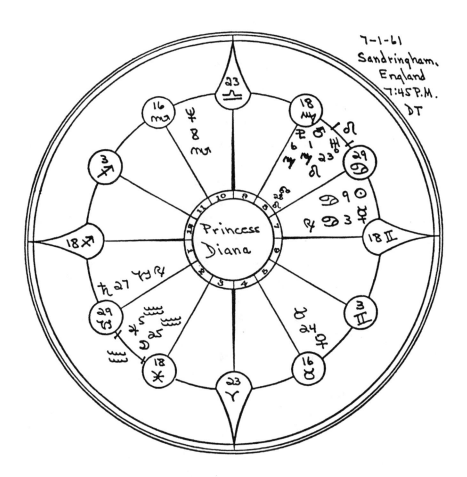

# PRINCE CHARLES

Prince Charles has a Leo Ascendant with Pluto (power) in the First House. Leo is the Sign of dignity and nobility. He has a "loaded" Fourth House with Sun, Mercury, Venus and Neptune placed there. This would make him a real home body. With eight of his Planets below the line, he would be introspective and introverted by nature. Mars and Jupiter are intercepted in Sagittarius in the Fifth House. Since the Fifth House represents recreation, and Sagittarius (the Centaur) has a connection with horses, Charles's love of horseback riding is very natural.

This is a very powerful Chart with one T Square and two Grand Trines. Despite his reticent nature, he will handle his responsibilities well with Mars and Pluto in Trine to each other, both Trining the Midheaven. His Taurus Moon is his Planet in highest ascendance, and is well placed in his Tenth House, forming a Grand Trine with Jupiter and Saturn. This adds greater strength to his ability to handle royal duties as England's future king. He can feel stress between his emotional responses as the Moon is in Opposition to Mercury, and both are squaring his Ascendant. This gives him problems in communicating warmly and easily. Mars Trine the Midheaven makes him willing to work for success. Mars Trine Pluto bestows leadership ability, usually indicating courage, ambition and the physical stamina to succeed. Pluto Trine the Midheaven gives drive for a successful career, plus constructive use of power. He has Aspects which could make him an excellent leader. Sun Square Pluto can cause feelings of frustration, but it also indicates executive ability.

With Venus Conjunct Neptune, Charles was seeking an ideal love, someone who would be his soul mate. Since his Venus is in Libra, he would be attracted to a woman with a prominent Libra placement. Princess Diana's Midheaven is in Libra. He needs a partner with a strong Aquarian influence in her Chart, as Aquarius is the Sign on his Seventh House partnership and marriage. Diana's Moon is in Aquarius.

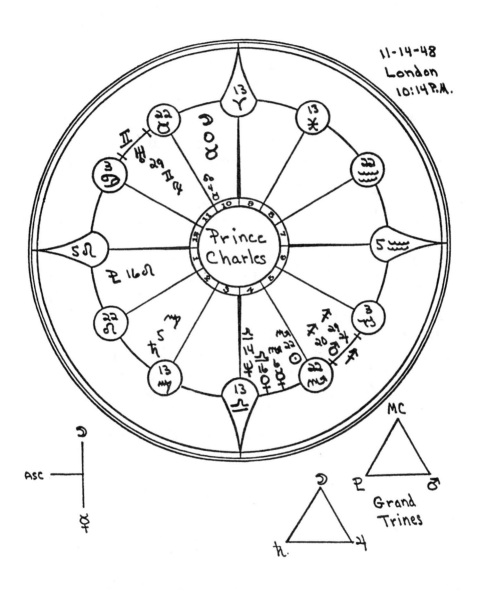

# MICHAEL JORDAN

Michael Jordan is a sports original. Uranus, the Planet of original-ity, is in his Fifth House (creativity, games/indoor sports). And to add power to the Fifth House, the Power Planet Pluto is also located there. The sign of Leo, the natural Ruler of the Fifth House, is on the Fifth House Cusp. Mars, the Action Planet, is fortunately located in Leo, the most creative Sign giving him creative energy. It's in the Fourth House, very close to the Fifth House Cusp. Pluto is extremely well Aspected. It is part of a Grand Trine with Venus in the Ninth House and the Ascendant. This is an Earth Grand Trine giving him strength and durability. He has a very physically strong Ascendant in Taurus. The symbol for Taurus is the Bull, and Michael is the star of the Chicago Bulls basketball team!

Michael is considered to be the greatest basketball player of all time. He can jump higher and stay in the air longer than any other player. He has an intuitive feel for making shots. He make shots "blind." He has a Trine between the Moon and Mars. The Moon represents the subcon-scious mind and Mars indicates our physical energy. So in a sense his body works well for him instinctively. Venus is in Capricorn in his Ninth House. This placement gives him a love of the higher abstract mind and Ninth House matters. Venus is Sextile Jupiter and Sextile Neptune. So his higher mind is strengthened by this Jupiter Aspect, and the involve-ment with Neptune greatly enhances his imagination. He imagines doing incredible things and does them.

Two other Planet Placements which benefit his career are the Sun in Aquarius (a popular Sign) in the Eleventh House (of friends, goals and popularity) and Mercury in Aquarius in the Tenth House, Conjunct the Midheaven. Mercury placed here is an asset in communicating. It is also the Planet in highest ascendancy giving it added importance in the Chart, and making it a great asset in his career.

While he is blessed with great talent, he does feel a lot of inner tension with three Inconjuncts. Mercury is Inconjunct (150° apart) Uranus; Venus is Inconjunct Mars; and Saturn is Inconjunct Pluto. Mars (his physical energy) is Square the Ascendant. One other Aspect which makes him feel more tension and gives him nervous energy is the Sun Opposition Uranus. So, he has the necessary friction Aspects to make him push for success.

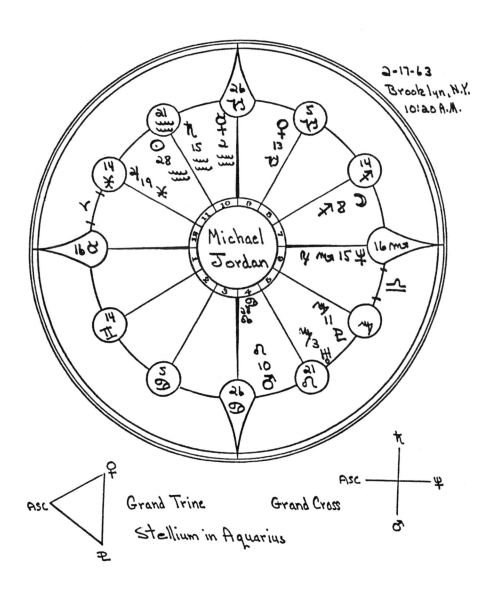

## GENERAL NORMAN SCHWARTZKOPF

In the Natal Chart of a prominent military person, there will be a strongly Aspected Mars. Mars rules weaponry. In ancient mythology, Mars was the god of war. General Schwartzkopf has the Power Planet Pluto in a very tight Conjunction with Mars. Conjunctions are the strongest Aspect. Mars is also Opposite his Moon, Square Jupiter, Square the Midheaven, and Inconjunct Saturn. Mars Square Jupiter in the Third House of communication is an indication of possible verbal explosions. The Mars-Pluto Conjunction also gives temper problems. With Sun, Mercury (in the First House) and his Ascendant all in Leo, there are powerful leadership qualities. With Venus in the Twelfth House, also in Leo, Conjunct his Ascendant, he would have an attractive personality. Saturn in his Seventh House is certainly indicative of the restrictions in his marriage partnership. With a military career, he did not have much time to spend with his partner.

With all of his natural leadership ability and his strongly Aspected Mars, what lifted him from a prominent military career to a great career? What made him a military genius? Uranus, the Planet of ingenuity and originality, is Conjunct his Midheaven! And very significantly, his Sun is Trine the Midheaven and Uranus Conjunction. Mercury is also Trine the Midheaven. So, there is a very harmonious flow of energy with these Trines. Eight of the Planets are on the left side of his Chart, giving him much control of his life. Uranus is his most elevated Planet, and therefore has even more significance.

His deep feeling emotions and his patriotism can be seen in his Mars-Pluto Conjunction in Cancer. Cancer is a deep feeling, patriotic Sign.

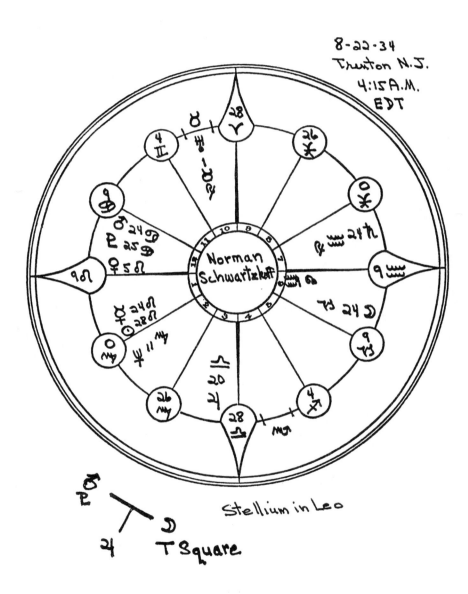

8-22-34
Trenton N.J.
4:15 A.M.
EDT

Norman
Schwartzkoff

Stellium in Leo

T Square

# 5

# Introduction to Intermediate Astrology

In learning astrology, Part II of this book is the most important section. Once that area is understood, there are many layers to add on to your knowledge. We'll look at three of them: Relationships, Career Indicators and Rectification. There are also books available on these individual topics.

## RELATIONSHIPS

We often talk about the chemistry between two people as something mysterious and intangible. A good astrologer should be able to look at two Charts (without seeing or knowing the people) and tell you whether there would be tremendous attraction between them or not. This ability to compare Charts is called "Synastry" or Chart comparison in astrology. There are many astrology books devoted entirely to this single subject of relationships.

As you become more secure in your understanding of astrology, you can do some Chart comparisons on your own. The easiest method is to take your Chart, and then on the outside of the Wheel, draw the Planets, Ascendant and Midheaven of the other person. It's a good idea to use a different color of ink for this. If you have a Virgo Ascendant, any Planet that the other person has in Virgo would be placed near your Ascendant. The exact position is dependent on the Degrees involved. You then look for any Aspects between your combined Planets, Ascendant, and Midheaven.

Contacts that involve the Sun, Moon, Venus or Mars to the other person's Ascendant show attraction, especially when the contact is by Trine, Sextile, or Conjunction. If the contact is by Square or Opposition, there can be attraction, but it will involve friction. (Proceed with caution!) Next, any ease contacts between any of the personal points and Planets will show attraction and harmony between the energy represented by the

Planets. The more Conjunctions, Trines and Sextiles involved, the stronger the attraction. Any contact to a First House Planet would be important.

In a woman's Chart, the Sign in which Mars is found shows the type of man a woman is attracted to. This does not necessarily mean that she will marry a man with this Sign. However, in a man's Chart, the Sign that his Venus falls in is a strong indication of the type of woman he'll marry. If his Venus Sign is the same as the Woman's Ascendant, Sun, or Moon, there will be a strong attraction. For example, my husband's Venus is in Pisces. My Ascendant is Pisces. So he is attracted to the way I look and my personality. His Sun is Sextile my Ascendant. His Mercury is Conjunct my First House Planet. His Ascendant is Conjunct my Jupiter and Pluto.

There are two House Cusps that have great importance in love and romance. The first is the Seventh House Cusp. This is the Marriage House. It indicates by the Sign on the Cusp what you need for balance in a partner. It is the opposition point to your Ascendant. The second important Cusp is the Fifth House. This is the House of love affairs and romance. I have Cancer on the Fifth House Cusp and my husband has a Cancer Ascendant. I have Virgo on the Seventh House Cusp and my husband has his Moon in Virgo. The more harmonious contacts that your Chart has with another, the smoother the relationship will be. With all the incredible favorable contacts that my Chart makes with my husband's, there was a problem area that I was able to resolve through my learning of astrology.

When I married for the second time, some years ago, I was determined that the marriage would be as "perfect" as possible. My husband and I are unbelievably compatible. We seldom have upsets or serious disagreements. When a disagreement would occur, I would be anxiously concerned until we could solve the problem. With a Sagittarian Sun, I am a very direct person, and I like to go right to the heart of the matter. For instance, I would try to straighten things out by saying what I thought had caused the disagreement — what I might have said to upset him, and explain what he had said to irritate me. The more I tried to solve things, the worse the situation would become. What had started as a ripple became a tidal wave.

It was through Jeanne Avery's book, <u>The Rising Sign, Your</u>

<u>Astrological Mask</u>, that the tidal waves disappeared. My husband's Sun, Moon and Mars are very apparent in his personality. I hadn't thought about his Cancer Ascendant very much because it wasn't pronounced. But when I read Jeanne Avery's description of the Cancer Ascendant, it changed our relationship dramatically. She says that Cancer Ascendant people are deeply emotional and sensitive. They are wonderful caring people, but when they are emotionally vulnerable, they go within their shell (like their symbol, the Crab). The more you try to get into contact with them, the more rigid the shell becomes. You must leave them alone until they regain their emotional equilibrium, come out of their shell, and are ready to talk with you. They still do not approach the problem in a direct way, but will sidle up to you in a sideways motion like a crab. While my direct Sagittarian approach had always worked well for me in the past, it was the worst method of problem solving with a Cancer Ascendant person. If there's an upset, I "give him his space" until he's ready to talk. So, thanks to my knowledge through astrology, there are only occasional ripples around our wonderfully happy relationship.

Relationships are studied in detail at the intermediate level of astrological study. An astrologer can do Chart comparisons for you. There are several fairly good computer programs for Chart comparisons now.

My favorite comic strip, Cathy, often deals with relationships. This is one of my favorites!

**cathy**                                              **by Cathy Guisewite**

# CAREER INDICATORS

There are many factors in a Chart that can be considered when looking for the right career. First and foremost is the location of your Sun by Sign and House, and then the Aspects to the Sun, showing what talents you can bring to bear to help you in your career. Your Sun shows the area by House location where you should strive to reach the highest — to do it to the max. The astrology textbooks list the varied careers that appeal to the different Signs.

When you look at your Trines and Sextiles, you will see talents and abilities that can greatly help your success. Some years ago, I took a large sheet of paper, and using Robert Pelletier's Planets in Aspect, I made a list of all the possible careers that my various Aspects indicated could be good for me. (You could also do this using a computerized interpretative Chart that includes Aspects.) When the same career or talent showed up again, I gave it an additional mark. Finally, five strong career indicators became very pronounced, with about four of five Aspects suggesting the same possible careers. Three of the career talents were already part of my history. The other two came as surprise — writing and research. I had not yet become a professional astrologer. Since then, I have been researching and writing articles for publication. I think this would be a very interesting experiment for anyone who would like to understand his/her full range of talents.

More career direction can be found from three of the Houses in your Natal Chart.

# CAREER INDICATORS FROM THE HOUSE CUSPS

There are three House Cusps to consider when looking toward a career. The Tenth House Cusp is also the Midheaven. It represents what we would like our public image to be. It shows the career we wish for and often achieve. The Sixth House Cusp shows what kind of work we do for a living. And the Second House Cusp represents our drive for self-earned income, and the talents or abilities we have to help us earn money. Any

Planets in these three Houses would give more clues as to how our ambitions can be realized. If the House or Houses are empty, we look to the Ruling Planet of the Sign on the Cusp. We take into consideration where this Planet is located and how it is Aspected.

# THE CAREER PLANET:  SATURN

Saturn is often referred to as the Career Planet because it is the natural Ruler of the Tenth House of career and public image. Saturn represents responsibility, restriction, discipline, boundaries, and business. The Sign in which Saturn is placed and its location by House give more information in career guidance. Its House location indicates where we want recognition. The Aspects to Saturn indicate the possibilities involved in a career. A well Aspected Saturn can indicate a prominent career. When Saturn is weak in a Chart, the career does not usually become prominent.

# CAREER INDICATORS FROM POWER PLANETS

Conjunctions to the Ascendant and Midheaven, besides giving power to a Chart, can give strong career indications. Any Planet in the First House, as well as the House location of the Sun, also give strong information toward careers. For instance, the Splash Chart sample is a man who was born in Milwaukee. He has Uranus at 27 Degrees of Pisces in the Tenth House Conjunct the Midheaven at 26 Degrees of Pisces. Uranus is the Planet of the scientist, the inventor, or the astrologer. This man is an inventor who is an industrial engineer/manufacturer. With the Sign Pisces involved, his products have a strong aesthetic influence. With his Sun in the Eleventh House, his career benefitted through friends.

The young man with a Bowl Shape Chart was born in Nashville. His Ascendant is at 5 Degrees, 31 Minutes of Virgo. He has the Planet Pluto in the First House at 5 Degrees, 34 Minutes of Virgo - an extremely tight and strong Conjunction. Pluto represents the Earth's underground and the underground of man's mind. The young man originally earned a college degree in geology. After graduation, he worked the night shift in a psychiatric hospital, and went back to college for two years in the daytime to earn a second degree. This degree was in psychology. He is now working toward a Ph.D. in psychology. So Pluto on this man's Ascendant manifested both in the underworld of the Earth and in the underworld of the mind. This man also has all his Planets below the Horizon Line, except Uranus, which is in the Twelfth House. Uranus is the Planet of the scientist, inventor, psychologist, and astrologer. Placed in the Twelfth House, he will work "behind the scenes" with people, possibly in an institution. From Chart emphasis, we know that his interests would be subjective and with invisible and spiritual matters. With his Sun and Moon in the Fifth, he will be creative in his work. And, since they are both in Aquarius, an Air Sign, he should be able to help people without becoming emotionally drained.

## THE SUN SIGN INFLUENCE IN CAREERS

People have often heard that the Sun Sign Pisces has many artists, actors and musicians born during that period. One of the surprises that I found researching the Sun Sign influence is that Pisces produces the largest number of prominent people. Paul Field, in his book, 50 Thousand Birthdays, took a random sample of over 8,000 people from Who's Who of American Biography over a 200 year period and recorded them by Sun Sign birth. The results showed that government services and/or public office, authors, educators and the clergy produced the greatest number of prominent people. The highest number were born during the Pisces period followed by Capricorn, Aquarius and Aries. The graph went straight down with the lowest number of prominent people born at the Cusp of Taurus and Gemini.

The graph line then went straight up to a smaller peak with Virgo followed by Libra. Then the line dips down again slightly to Scorpio and starts climbing again through Sagittarius to the second highest peak of Capricorn.

In studies of individual careers, Mr. Field found that the greatest number of airplane pilots in two studies showed the highest peak was reached in the Sign Aquarius, followed by Libra, then Aries in a third peak.

The most prominent achievement in chemistry was found among the Libras, with a second peak in Taurus and Gemini. It should be noted that the adjacent Signs to the Sign in the highest peak would also be at a high level. Pisces produced a dramatically high peak from over 7,000 people listed in a <u>Who's Who of Music</u>. The warm weather periods of Gemini, Cancer and Leo produced the greatest number of lawyers, with the second peak in Scorpio. Leos were the highest peak found among sea captains. The highest number of senators and representatives were found to be Capricorns, with a second peak in Pisces. Virgo had the highest peak among surgeons, followed by Capricorn in the second peak and Cancer in the third peak.

## SUN SIGN INFLUENCE IN CAREERS

| Career | Highest Peak | Next Highest Peak | Lowest Peak | # People In Study |
|---|---|---|---|---|
| Pilots Air Force & Navy Fighters | Aquarius | Libra Aries | Gemini | 10,000 |
| Chemists | Libra | Taurus Gemini | Sagittarius Cancer | 7,500 |
| Musicians | Pisces | (none) | Virgo | 7,000 |
| Lawyers | Gemini | Leo Cancer Scorpio | Aquarius | 7,000 |
| Sea Captains | Leo | Pisces | Aquarius | 2,000 |
| Senators Represent- atives | Capricorn | Pisces | Taurus Cancer | 4,000 |
| Surgeons | Virgo | Capricorn | Taurus | 2,000 |

It's important to note that the Signs adjacent to the peaks would also have a high number of people in that career. The source for these statistics is <u>50 Thousand Birthdays</u> by Paul Field. Mr. Field shows the Zodiac influence in many more different categories in his book.

# ⟋RECTIFICATION

When the time of birth is not known, there is a procedure in astrology used to try to find the time. This procedure is called Chart Rectification. Rectification tries to place the Planets in what appears to be their House locations, and tries to put the correct Sign on the Ascendant. After experimenting with many possibilities, if the pieces seem to fit, the Rectified Chart is then put to the test of major events in that person's life, by Transits and Progressions.

This brings us to the second major part of astrology. The first part is the Natal Chart which gives you your psychological profile. The second part of astrology (which is studied in an intermediate course) is involved with Transits and Progressions. Transits mean that the continuing movement of the Planets can show contacts (through transiting Aspects) throughout our life. These contacts can signal periods of various cycles in our life — such as periods of good health versus periods to guard against health problems, or the opportune time to earn good money versus the time to be careful and thrifty with your money. Transits do not tell you exactly what will happen in your life, but only indicate trends so that you can be alert to opportunities, or know when to be careful.

Progressions are also called Directions. Their influence is usually much more subtle than Transits. Progressions are symbolic movement. A progression moves the Planets one day (as their motion is listed in an ephemeris) for a year of your life. So at age 21, the Progressed Planets would be in the same Planetary positions that they were in 21 days after your birth. For example, if you had the Planet Venus at 17 Degrees of Pisces on the day you were born (as the Milwaukee man with the Splash Chart has), 21 days later Venus (a fast moving Planet) would be at 9 Degrees of Aries. So at 21 years of age, the Progressed Venus would be at 9 Degrees of Aries. Progressions are supposed to show growth directions in your life. This is a brief explanation of a complex subject that is usually taught in an eight-week course. I offer it here to let people know, who are anxious to have their Charts Rectified, how it works.

There are many different approaches to Rectification. I'm presenting my method which was published by the American Federation of Astrologers in their monthly bulletin in September of 1984.

Chart Rectification is very exciting to me. While it's time consuming and difficult, I think it is a fascinating part of astrology. The approach to Rectification that works well for me begins with an assumption on my part. For instance, in trying to determine the time of birth in my father's Chart, I began by placing the Sun in the Third House. He was the beloved sibling of all his brothers and sisters in a very large family. Isabel Hickey describes this as the Sun's House Placement when there is much love received from brothers and sisters. With no Gemini emphasis in his Chart, he had a passion for mundane communication. He read two newspapers every day, and loved to read out-of-town papers, which the family would always bring home from trips for him.

He was also an outstanding communicator. The placement of the Sun in the Third House let his other Planets fall in appropriate Houses, and gave him an Aquarian Ascendant, which seemed to fit his personality. Aquarians are very interested in new and unusual things. One of my Dad's favorite expressions was "It's as modern as tomorrow!" These two locations (of the Sun and Ascendant) placed Neptune in his Sixth House. Remember that Neptune is the Planet of idealism and illusion or disillusion. My father was a lawyer who "ideally" wanted to help the underdog. He became a criminal lawyer and practiced law for several years. But he became disillusioned by the fact that the same people came back time and again for the same crimes. He changed careers and spent the rest of his life in sales, where his Third House Sun could shine, with lots of communication and many short trips! From that point, I worked with the major Transits of his life to find the exact Degree on the Ascendant.

With a friend whose time of birth was unknown, I began with the assumption that he had Capricorn rising. He is a biology professor who looks like an El Greco painting of one of the Apostles. He has a thin, bony face. Capricorn rules the bones and people with Capricorn rising usually are slender with facial bones that are very prominent. So I chose an Ascendant that matched his looks. We tend to look like our Ascendant Sign description. The House overlay pattern seemed to work as well as the Planet placement. (House overlay pattern means how the Signs on the Twelfth House Cusps fit the description of the person. If the Ascending Sign is correct, the next 11 Signs will accurately suit that person). His career cycles fit the Chart as well.

In my attempt to determine my mother's birth time, I tried

important and seemingly obvious placement of two of her Planets. She had a lifelong interest in law (a Ninth House subject) and she was a highly intelligent lady, so I placed her Sun in the Ninth House. This Rectification was aided by a traumatic event in her life, when at age 14, her own mother died. This showed in the Chart by Progressions of her Sun to the Midheaven.

Recently, a friend of mine told me that there is nothing she likes better than beating someone on a golf course. I asked her if she had been born between 8:00 and 10:00 P.M. (this would place her Sun in the Fifth House of fun and games). She checked her birth time for me, and I had guessed right. Remember that where our Sun is, is where we want to shine our light the brightest. She is a Taurus, and she has the athletic Sign of Sagittarius on her Ascendant. So, a clue like that can give an astrologer a good start in attempting to Rectify a Chart.

One verification that many astrologers use to read the correct time of birth is the Transits of Uranus to the House Cusps. Uranus takes 84 years to orbit the Sun, so it usually hits each House only once. Uranus is the revolutionary Planet that forces change. Uranus transits to my House Cusps have run like clockwork throughout my life.

Before I was finally able to get my stepson's birth time, I worked on his Chart Rectification. He has incredible energy. You can feel his live-wire energy when you're in the same room with him. I thought of an Aries Ascendant because of their intense energy but discarded it because he did not have an aggressive Aries personality. When I obtained his birth time, I found that he does have an Aries connection on the Ascendant though, because Mars (the Ruler of Aries) is in his First House, Conjunct the Ascendant.

If you know a person who is still bitter and vengeful ten years after a divorce, that's a strong signal to place Scorpio on the Ascendant! An Ascendant to think of with someone who is a stylish dresser is Virgo. These people usually know how to put it all together. Virgos also are youthful in appearance.

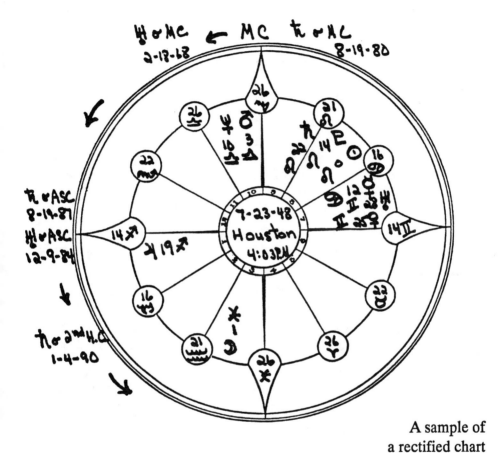

A sample of
a rectified chart

The motion of the planets is always counter clockwise. Transits of Uranus and Saturn are listed outside the wheel. These transits were used to help rectify this woman's chart. She is a personnel director, so that Mars and Neptune in the public relations sign of Libra, placed in the career 10 th House, is very appropriate. She is also an excellent tennis player, so that Jupiter Conjunct the Ascendant in Sagittarius is also a good indicator of a correct placement.

Attorneys often have their Sun or Mercury in the Eighth House. This is the in-depth House, so there would be an interest in digging to the bottom of things. The Bowl shaped Chart from Washington, D.C. belongs to a young woman attorney. She has both her Sun, Moon and Mercury in the Eighth. The Sling Chart from Syracuse, New York belongs to a man who is also an attorney. He has Sun, Venus and Pluto in the Eighth. The Bucket shaped Chart from Pittsburgh belongs to a woman who is a corporate vice president of a broadcasting company. She has the Sun, Mars and Neptune in the Third House of communications — a perfect placement for her career. A friend who is a successful businessman has his Sun and Mercury in the Seventh House of partnership. He likes to work in business partnerships rather than on his own. These are just a few examples of how Planet placement by House can help give clues in Chart rectification.

The physical appearance of a person often gives clues to the Ascending Sign. Water Sign Ascending people have a watery film on their eyes. Scorpio Ascendants, or someone with Scorpio's ruling Planet Pluto Conjunct the Ascendant, can have "bedroom eyes." Very bony people often have Capricorn rising. Women with Pisces Ascendants are usually very feminine and tend to have pear-shaped figures. There are several books which describe many of the physical characteristics frequently seen in the different Ascendants.

A major test for a rectified Chart is to try an overlay pattern on what is thought to be the correct Chart. An overlay pattern means which twelve Signs fit on the House Cusps of the Chart, starting with the Ascendant. These Signs should fit the description of the person in the rectified Chart. The two textbooks recommended under learning tips have excellent descriptions of the twelve different overlay patterns.

And now on to a sample of a rectified Chart. The first time that I saw Ronald Reagan's Natal Chart, I challenged its validity. It was presented in an advanced astrology class many years ago. The instructor informed the class that only the approximate time of birth was known. The Chart showed Scorpio rising. Since none of the Planets were in Fire

Signs, I felt strongly that he would have a Fire Sign Ascendant, and I thought it would be in Sagittarius. His outgoing, friendly, cheerful personality seems to fit that rising Sign. The single most important quality that Fire Signs have is enthusiasm. This is a quality that Mr. Reagan has so it must show up somewhere in his Chart, and I thought it should be prominent. The Charts I've worked on with Sagittarius rising have usually shown tremendous physical energy, and a quick optimistic response to people, which Reagan has. Because Ronald Reagan does not have any Planets in Fire Signs, if he did not have a Fire Sign Ascendant, he would lack enthusiasm and self esteem — two qualities that he has in good measure. So, my first clue to this Chart was to try to place Sagittarius on the Ascendant.

After assuming that Ronald Reagan had Sagittarius rising, I started checking his career cycles. I have found that Saturn cycles as described in the late Don Jacobs' (Moby Dick) book on Transits to be wonderfully helpful in pinpointing birth times.

Briefly, Saturn has a 29 1/2 year orbit of the Sun. Since Saturn is the career Planet, Jacobs divides Saturn's Transit through the Constellations into four 7 1/3 year segments. The first segment begins at the Fourth House Cusp and extends to the Seventh. He calls this the period of building, when a person is working in a new career, or is going in a new direction in the same career. Segment two is from the Seventh to the Tenth House Cusp and is called the period of triumph — this is when the 7 years of building start paying off. The career peak occurs when Saturn reaches the Tenth House (approximately) 14 years from the point on the IC. I've been clipping articles about well-known people for several years showing this career peak ever since Don Jacobs taught this theory to me. The third segment goes from the Tenth to the First House Cusp. This is called the period of coasting. Once you've put 14 years into building your success, you stay at the top from the momentum (as if you were coasting on a bicycle after pumping hard). The fourth and final segment is from the First House Cusp to the Fourth. This is the period of obscurity. This is the period where many celebrities fade from view, until they start the cycle over again. I tell students not to worry about having to wait 30 years for a career peak because they also will have a solar peak (with Saturn in upper Square to their Sun).

According to Don Jacobs' theory of Saturn cycles, Ronald Reagan should have had transiting Saturn in lower Square to his Ascendant (near the IC) when he began his two major, different careers. My rectification of the Chart put 18 Degrees of Sagittarius on the Ascendant and Aries on the Fourth House Cusp. The lower Square occurred when Saturn reached 18 Degrees of Pisces in 1937, the year President Reagan made his film debut. Saturn was again in later Degrees of Pisces when Mr. Reagan was first elected to public office as governor of California in 1967 thus beginning a new career in politics. The Jacobs' theory of career change is within a year of the Saturn lower Square to the Ascendant. When Mr. Reagan was elected president of the Screen Actors Guild in 1947, transiting Saturn was Trine his rectified Ascendant and Jupiter was transiting his Eleventh House (both strong indicators that my rectified Chart was correct).

From this point, I next looked at his two marriages. If I had the angles of his Chart figured correctly, I thought his marriage would be indicated by progression. When he married Jane Wyman on January 25, 1940, his progressed Venus was approaching a Conjunction to his Fourth House Cusp (of the home) within one Degree. When he courted Nancy Davis, his progressed Moon transited his Natal Jupiter (a very fortunate progression) and his progressed Ascendant was Conjunct his Natal Uranus when he married her in 1952.

To further verify the exact Degree of his Ascendant, I chose to look at the transits on the day the president was shot. I zeroed in on this Degree with the transit of Uranus on March 31, 1981. Uranus was at 29 Degrees of Scorpio, Conjunct his rectified Twelfth House Cusp (the house of hidden enemies). On that day, the transiting Sun and Mars were Conjunct his Fourth House Cusp (which signifies the beginning and ending of life. Sun and Mars transiting here are vital signs of life). Mercury was Conjunct his Part of Fortune. (This is an Arabian Part indicating a lucky point).

My rectified Chart places Pisces — the actor's Sign — on Mr. Reagan's Third House Cusp of communication. This would give him great appeal as a communicator. Since the Third House Cusp indicates the type of mind we have, Pisces here for Mr. Reagan is very significant. While he is not thought of as a scholarly person, he is said to have an almost photographic mind (Pisces influence) which helped him greatly as a student.

My rectified Chart places Mercury and Mars in his First House, an appropriate placement for so vital a person for his age, with quick recuperative powers.

Another test of the validity of my rectified Chart for Mr. Reagan would be the fact that transiting Saturn had been going through his Twelfth House (of hospitalization) during the period of his cancer surgery. My rectified Chart shows Scorpio on his Twelfth House Cusp. Scorpio rules the bladder. Mr. Reagan has had surgery to remove stones from his bladder. And he has had bladder problems for the past twenty years.

The placement of his Ascendant at 18 Degrees of Sagittarius puts Libra on his Midheaven, giving him an attractive public image. It also puts the Ruling Planet of his Chart (Jupiter, the luckiest Planet) in the Eleventh House (of popularity) where it's proved very beneficial for him.

One final note, on this rectification, is that when he ascended to the presidency in January of 1981, transiting Saturn was Conjunct his Midheaven of 10 Degrees Libra. Saturn Conjunct the Midheaven always signifies a career peak. Another book that is very helpful in rectification is Robert Hand's Planets in Transit. His description of Saturn Conjunct the Midheaven and transiting the Tenth House gave me further assurance that I had figured the rectified Chart correctly.

In 1989, Joan Quigley published her book, "What Does Joan Say?: My Seven Years as White House Astrologer to Nancy and Ronald Reagan." This was five years after my article on Ronald Reagan's rectified Chart was published. I was pleased to read that this prominent astrologer had rectified the Chart to the same Degree of Sagittarius on the Ascendant that I had selected.

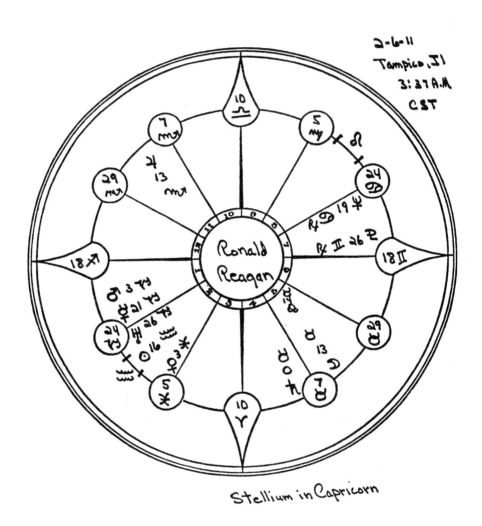

Stellium in Capricorn

RONALD REAGAN
Rectified Birth Time
(exact time unknown)

# Reference
# Section

This section is not meant to be read from beginning to end (although it certainly may be if that is your style of reading). It should be used when studying an individual Chart. For example, if it is your own Chart, select the section which describes your Planets in the appropriate Signs and Houses. Then read the Aspects that apply to your Planets. It really brings the information home if you would copy the descriptions of your Planets in Signs, Houses and Aspects in sequence in your own handwriting. This will give you a quick reference to your Chart. It will help you understand your talents and strengths, so that you can use them to the fullest.

# THE PLANETS IN THE SIGNS

## THE MOON IN THE SIGNS

|  | Emotional Nature | Emotional Personality | Emotional Needs |
|---|---|---|---|
| Aries | Fiery<br>Enthusiastic<br>Restless<br>Impulsive<br>Passionate<br>Spontaneous<br>Uncomplicated | Independent<br>Aggressive<br>Competitive<br>Quick-tempered<br>Dynamic<br>Candid<br>Self-centered | Freedom<br>Excitement<br>To win<br>To take chances<br>Immediate<br>To be liked |
| Taurus | The most stable<br>Practical<br>Methodical<br>Patient<br>Resists change<br>Strong, loyal | Slow to anger<br>Conservative<br>Determined<br>Content<br>Deep feeling<br>Affectionate | Security in the<br>home, money<br>Stability<br>Artistic connec-<br>tion, either<br>active or passive<br>Possessions<br>Touching |
| Gemini | Intellectual,<br>likes to talk<br>about love<br>rather than<br>feel it<br>Surface only,<br>lacking depth<br>Self-expressive<br>Problems<br>integrating<br>thoughts and<br>emotions | Versatile<br>Alert<br>Talkative<br>High-strung<br>Friendly<br>Changeable<br>Restless | Recognition<br>People<br>Love of music<br>Pleasure in read-<br>ing and writing<br>Variety<br>Mobility |

| Cancer | Powerful | Sensitive | Family |
|--------|----------|-----------|--------|
| | Deep, intense | Sympathetic | Home |
| | Nurturing | Romantic | Children |
| | Psychic | Social | Love |
| | Fluctuating moods | Imaginative | Security |
| | beneath the | Intuitive | Marriage |
| | surface | Very giving | intimacy |
| | Vulnerable | | |
| | Caring, tenacious | | |
| | | | |
| Leo | Warm | Confident | Attention |
| | Enthusiastic | Charming | Success |
| | Noble | Dramatic | Pleasure |
| | Giving | Dignified | Respect |
| | Kind | Imaginative | The spotlight |
| | Self-centered | Flirtatious | Romance |
| | | | |
| Virgo | Practical | Critical | Service/work |
| | Analytical | Helpful | Top quality in |
| | Picky toward | Reserved | work |
| | loved one | Unassuming | Wants to be in |
| | Industrious | Skeptical | control |
| | Conservative | | Good hygiene |
| | Sees things in | | |
| | black and white | | |
| | | | |
| Libra | Refined | Charming | Beauty |
| | Idealistic | Cooperative | Partner who gives |
| | Romantic | Social | intellectual |
| | Self-indulgent | Courteous | love |
| | Surface only, | Indecisive | Security |
| | unless forced to | Responsive | Harmony |
| | probe inward | | Attractive/active |
| | | | social life |
| | | | |
| Scorpio | Secretive | Intense | Self understanding |
| | Powerful | Probing | Secure love |
| | Deep, biased | Magnetic | relationship |
| | | | Wants perfection |

|              | Controlled | Complex | To dominate |
|              | Self-reliant | Problems with anger | Power |
|              | Intuitive | Compassionate | Crises |
|              | Fiercely | Can be jealous | |
|              | determined | | |
|              | Passionate | | |

| Sagittarius | Independent | Enthusiastic | Exploring, ment- |
|             | Expansive | Witty | ally and physi- |
|             | Warm | Outspoken | cally |
|             | Intuitive | Cheerful | Humor |
|             | Idealistic | Spontaneous | To travel |
|             | Generous | Charming | Freedom |
|             | Daring | Helpful | To be right |

| Capricorn | Ambitious | Cautious | Financial security |
|           | Disciplined | Serious | Material goods |
|           | Dutiful | Structured | Appreciation |
|           | Reserved | Oversensitive | A long lasting, |
|           | Inhibited | Vulnerable | serious love |
|           | Cool | Pessimistic | Status |
|           | Melancholy | Superior attitude | |

| Aquarius | Very detached | Unconventional | Friends |
|          | Cool | Clever | Community |
|          | Independent | Imaginative | Idealism |
|          | Nervous, tense | Social | Goals |
|          | Intellectual | Understanding | To help mankind |
|          | Loyal | Impersonal | Freedom |

| Pisces | Deep feeling | Responsive | To help others |
|        | Sensitive | Sympathetic, | Escapism some |
|        | Powerful | Kind, Loving | times |
|        | imagination | Complex | Spiritual goals |
|        | Courageous | Dependent | To see only good |
|        | Idealistic | Gentle | in the world |
|        | Susceptible | Non-materialistic | |
|        | Psychic, intuitive | Complex | |
|        | Self-sacrificing | | |

# MERCURY IN THE SIGNS

| | Type of mentality | Mental Expression | Ability |
|---|---|---|---|
| Aries | Decisive<br>Quick<br>Alert<br>Sees things in<br>black and white | Assertive<br>Competitive<br>Direct<br>Can be combative<br>"Butts in" | Original ideas<br>Clever |
| Taurus | Practical<br>Strong concentration,<br>like tunnel vision<br>Slow decisions | Slow and deliberate<br>Can be diplomatic | In business and<br> finance<br>In the arts with form<br> or structure<br>Shrewd manager |
| Gemini | Active<br>Versatile<br>Unbiased<br>Fact-Oriented<br>Agile | Rapid<br>Precise<br>Fluid<br>Witty<br>Detached | Great original<br>thinking in problem<br>solving<br>Communication<br>skills<br>Science/Math |
| Cancer | Clear perceptions,<br>which can become<br>subjective<br>Emotionally sensitive<br>Good planner | Imaginative<br>Interesting<br>Easily influenced | In Fourth House<br>matters food, home<br>furnishings,<br>real estate<br>Good Memory |
| Leo | Creative<br>Focused mental<br>energy, sees the<br>big scene, but<br>not details<br>Ambitious | Dramatic<br>Confident<br>Enthusiastic<br>"The Boss"<br>Diginified | Acting<br>Speaking<br>Teaching |
| Virgo | Logical<br>Practical<br>Analytical<br>Common sense<br>Narrowly focused | Meticulous<br>Critical<br>Systematic<br>Overly intellectual | In speech and writing<br>Precision work<br>In mental games<br>Manual dexterity<br>Research |

| Libra | Well balanced<br>Good reasoning<br>Able to see both<br>sides of a problem<br>Aesthetically inclined | Smooth<br>Refined<br>Diplomatic<br>Judgmental | Often in public rela-<br>tions, psychology,<br>law or astrology<br>In the Arts<br>Debating |
| --- | --- | --- | --- |
| Scorpio | Penetrating<br>Shrewd<br>Secretive<br>Resourceful | Persuasive<br>Positive | Psychology/Psychiatry<br>Investigating |
| Sagittarius | Ethical<br>Exploring<br>Lacking in focus<br>and concentration<br>Sees the forest, but<br>not the trees<br>Dislike of details<br>Intuitive | Direct<br>Cheerful<br>Impatient<br>Impulsive<br>Honest<br>Humorous | To inspire<br>Acute perception |
| Capricorn | Methodical<br>Analytical<br>Ambitious<br>Good memory<br>Well organized<br>Disciplined<br>Sharp | Precise<br>Uncluttered<br>Serious<br>Diplomatic<br>Resourceful | Business mind<br>Managerial ability |
| Aquarius | Clever, inventive<br>Detached<br>Creative<br>Intellectual<br>Penetrating<br>Independent | Original<br>Accurate<br>Pleasant<br>Logical<br>Impersonal<br>Honest | In science, math or<br>astrology<br>Creative<br>Wit |
| Pisces | Psychic, intuitive<br>Receptive<br>Photographic<br>Witty<br>Imaginative<br>Absent-minded | Subtle<br>Vivid<br>Sensitive<br>Gentle<br>Refined<br>Shy | Artistic<br>Creative<br>Musical or math skills |

**VENUS IN THE SIGNS**

# Venus in the Signs

|  | Sociability | Love Nature | Sensuality |
|---|---|---|---|
| Aries | Assertive<br>Likeable<br>Outgoing<br>Extravagant | Impulsive<br>Affectionate<br>Competitive<br>Self-centered | Ardent<br>Fiery<br>Passionate |
| Taurus | Warm<br>Pleasant<br>Generous<br>Easygoing | Long lasting<br>Deep<br>Self indulgent<br>Affectionate | Strong<br>Very physical<br>Strong sense of touch |
| Gemini | Good disposition<br>Outgoing<br>Witty<br>Spontaneous | Likes variety -<br>the butterfly<br>Attractive<br>Flirtatious | Intellectual<br>Light touch<br>Refined |
| Cancer | Pleasant<br>Gentle<br>Sensitive<br>Home oriented | Devoted<br>Romantic<br>Nurturing<br>Possessive<br>Deep | Strong need for love<br>Imaginative but needs<br>privacy |
| Leo | Popular<br>Pleasure loving<br>Dramatic<br>Needs approval | Generous<br>Likes to be<br>center of atten-<br>tion<br>Creative<br>Proud | Spontaneous<br>Warm<br>Affectionate, touching |
| Virgo | Discriminating<br>Likes routines<br>Work oriented | Detached, avoids<br>intimacy<br>Fastidious<br>Undemonstrative<br>Non romantic<br>Secretive | Controlled<br>Can be sublimated<br>Conventional |

Note: There are more single women with Venus in Virgo because "no one quite comes up to their perfection."

| Libra | Charming | Very loving | Refined |
| --- | --- | --- | --- |
| | Outgoing | Tender | Romantic |
| | Dignified | Harmonious | Great need for love but |
| | Attractive to the | Affectionate | not shown in public |
| | opposite sex | | |
| | Avoids conflict | | |
| | | | |
| Scorpio | Emotional response | Passionate | Extremely sensual |
| | to people | Profound | Strong need for sexual |
| | Sensitive | Subtle | expression |
| | Intriguing, | Possessive | |
| | interesting | Proud | |
| | personality | | |
| | | | |
| Sagittarius | Humorous | Impulsive | Warm |
| | Self confident | Direct | Spontaneous |
| | Adventurous | Sincere | Exuberant |
| | Interesting | Romantic | |
| | | | |
| Capricorn | Serious | Repressed | Discreet |
| | Ambitious | Disciplined | Cool in public, can be |
| | Can be melancholy | Long lasting | lusty in private |
| | They seek important | Self interest | Private |
| | people to help | | |
| | their success | | |
| | | | |
| Aquarius | Magnetic | Detached | Unconventional |
| | personality | Impersonal | Suddenly aroused |
| | Talkative | Cool | |
| | Likes people in | Idealistic | |
| | general, but | | |
| | not "too close" | | |
| | | | |
| Pisces | Aesthically tuned | Very giving | Extremely tender and |
| | Compassionate | Too generous | loving |
| | Sensitive | Non-judgemental | Romantic |
| | Emotional | Great capacity for | Refined |
| | | love which often | |
| | | involves suffering | |

# MARS IN THE SIGNS

|  | Type of Energy | Drive | Ability | Sexuality |
|---|---|---|---|---|
| Aries | Aggressive<br>Tremendous energy<br>Courageous<br>Athletic<br>Good physical<br>strength | Quick<br>Direct<br>Impulsive<br>Competitive<br>Independent | Mechanical<br>Likes cars<br>and machines | Fiery<br>Strong<br>Quick |
| Taurus | Steady<br>Controlled<br>Good stamina | Practical<br>Determined<br>Persistent<br>Sensual | Craftsman,<br>with tools | Earthy<br>Sensuous |
| Gemini | Off and on<br>Nervous<br>Assertive | Changeable<br>Restless<br>Intellectual | Communica-<br>tions: writing<br>Manual dex-<br>terity | Sometimes on,<br>other times<br>off<br>Likes variety |
| Cancer | Emotional<br>Moody<br>Non aggressive<br>(hides anger) | Indirect<br>(like a crab)<br>Ambitious<br>To control the<br>home | Imagination<br>Good memory<br>To hold on in<br>Fourth House<br>areas | Strong<br>Emotional |
| Leo | Creative<br>Strong willed<br>Focused | Powerful<br>Enthusiastic<br>Stable<br>Competitive | Strong<br>personality<br>Leadership<br>Acting | Passionate<br>Impulsive<br>Strongly<br>attracted to the<br>opposite sex |
| Virgo | Disciplined<br>Efficient<br>Problems with<br>anger | Sustained, hard<br>working<br>Analytical | Practical<br>Craftsmanship<br>in detailed<br>work | Can be<br>sublimated |
| Libra | Balanced, well<br>controlled | Social<br>Cooperative<br>For justice | Persuasive<br>To conciliate<br>Artistic | Refined<br>Can be<br>sublimated |

| | | | | |
|---|---|---|---|---|
| Scorpio | Determined<br>Disciplined | Magnetic<br>Fierce<br>Self-reliant<br>For power | To investigate | Highly sexed<br>Passionate |
| Sagittarius | Fiery, therefore<br>burns out<br>Enthusiastic<br>Self-confident | Broad<br>Courageous<br>Fast | Outdoor sports<br>Lusty | Spontaneous |
| Capricorn | Systematic<br>Persistent<br>Conscientious<br>Well-timed | Hard working<br>toward success<br>Ambitious<br>Practical<br>Controlled | In organization<br>and management | Earthy<br>Passionate |
| Aquarius | Nervous<br>Impulsive<br>Dynamic | Intellectual<br>For change and<br>revolution | Creative<br>originality<br>Inventive | Detached<br>Unusual or<br>offbeat |
| Pisces | Sluggish<br>Comes and goes | For spiritual<br>purpose<br>Non-combative<br>Lacks direction | In the arts | Sensual |

# JUPITER IN THE SIGNS
**Jupiter is in each Sign for approximately one year.**

## Aries

Jupiter expands the Aries traits of leadership, enthusiasm, courage and daring. There is tremendous self-confidence. There is an impulsive, risk-taking nature. There is a love of action and speed to match the great energy of this placement. These people are best suited to active type jobs. There is a strong tendency to optimistically think and plan big, with a dislike of thorough detail planning. This can be a problem, unless there is help elsewhere in the Chart to balance this tendency. This combination of Planet and Sign often produces pioneers. There is an intense love of fun and pleasurable social activities, which needs to be checked, so that it isn't carried to extreme. There is such a strong need for freedom, that these people can seem rebellious at times. There is a depth of original thinking.

## Taurus

When Jupiter is in Taurus, there is ability in the Taurean areas of money management and ownership of land. The Taurus love of beautiful possessions is expanded. Luxury and material things are emphasized. They must guard against extravagance. There is the ability for long, hard work. Managerial skills are usually quite pronounced. This combination increases the Taurean trait of generosity. It also strengthens the stubbornness of the Taurus mind. While the mind is geared toward good practical thinking, there is an absence of original ideas.

## Gemini

Jupiter enhances the Gemini characteristics of sociability and versatility. Cleverness is often pronounced. These people seem to always be "on the go." Communication skills are usually very good. There is often writing ability. If it's in fiction, the talent for developing plots can be ingenious. The problems with this placement include the possibility of scattering the energies too much and possible nervous irritability. The latter may not be apparent to others because of the natural charm that this combination produces. There is intense curiosity. These people are usually the center of attention in social situations, and they thrive on it.

### Cancer

The nurturing instincts are very pronounced with Jupiter in Cancer people. They usually put their families at the center of their universe. They are hard workers in making their homes attractive and safe. The Cancer areas of food and interior design are often gifted with this combination. These are the people who enjoy entertaining in their homes. Their imaginations are very good and active, and yet practical. With Jupiter here, there is a wealth of good feeling toward others. The disposition is usually cheerful and kind. Since Cancer involves business ability, Jupiter here would enlarge their judgment in business situations. The emotions are extremely pronounced. The liabilities with this placement include a love of food, which can cause weight problems, and a tendency to hold onto things because of emotional ties. This is one of the two best placements for Jupiter. Intuition is powerful here. There is a natural ability to influence the public.

### Leo

The self-confidence of Leo is expanded and reinforced when Jupiter is here. Since Leo is the Sign of leadership, Jupiter will make the leader popular. Dramatic flair and love of display are most pronounced. While the ego is often very apparent, it is not inflated. These people can do what they say they can do! The Leo love of being in the spotlight is intensified. There is a fierce desire to be very prominent, and this is not based on financial reward. The Leo characteristics of nobility, vitality, good humor and affection are increased. Since Leo is the Sign of creativity, Jupiter brings good luck and increased talent in the areas of self-expression. Romances are grand passions. A note of caution should be used to avoid appearing snobbish or too vain. There is concern for the welfare of mankind.

### Virgo

The Virgo attention to detail is expanded by Jupiter's placement here. There is a talent for technical matters and research. These people want to accumulate knowledge to utilize it. The Virgo characteristics of work and service are enlarged. Their capacity for handling minutely detailed jobs is amazing. Their talent and ability are applied to their work situations, while their daily living can be quite ordinary. They can be too work-oriented, and be lacking in the social graces (unless there is help elsewhere in the Chart). There can be a problem with being too critical and becoming narrow-minded. This combination can produce a skeptical attitude toward religion. There is often pronounced writing talent in intellectual, and/or scientific areas. They often make good troubleshooters in problem solving manufacturing or technical difficulties. They love to learn practical things with their alert minds.

### Libra

The natural tendencies of Libra to socialize and be pleasing to other people are greatly emphasized when Jupiter is in this Sign. These people usually make very good judges, with a fine sense of justice. They are often very prominent in the legal professions. They also can achieve great success in politics, government and large corporations. They have a knack for making good social contacts. They try so hard to please because there is a strong dislike of conflict. They seem to have the ability to avoid most confrontations, even at the last moment. The greatest success usually comes in partnership. The need for partnership is often so pronounced, that there can be a lack of independence. The artistic tendencies of Libra are enhanced. These people often have exquisite taste. They love to go "first class." When the artistic side of Libra is more pronounced than the legal side, you will find these people in careers of adornment and beauty. A drawback of this placement can be too much enjoyment of pleasure and comfort, so that they can become lazy (unless other Planets provide the drive). Jupiter in Libra people can elevate hospitality to an art.

### Scorpio

The Scorpio qualities of willpower and skill in research and investigation are very prominent. Careers in undercover work or psychology are usually very successful. This combination instills so much self-confidence that these people have to guard against pride. Jupiter here tends to bring balance to the intensity of Scorpio. There is a fierce drive for success and power. Natural ability in business is often pronounced. There is a desire for material things. Scorpio's interest in sex is intense, and there is desire for new and varied sensations. There can be an interest in using drugs and alcohol to this end. But there is usually the capacity to control the use of these things. With the Scorpio interest in occult matters, Jupiter can enlarge this interest, and bring far-seeing insight into the psychic arena.

### Sagittarius

This is a very fortunate placement. It is especially benefical for the mind. The intellect can frequently be developed to the fullest. There is often ability in literature, or law, or philosophy. People with this placement are usually extremely optimistic and generous. There is often a love of the outdoors and outdoor sports. This position is an indicator of success, unless there are restrictions elsewhere in the Chart. This combination gives the ability to see far-ranging goals, as well as immediate opportunities. It produces people who are able to direct others successfully. There is intense love of, and need for, freedom. The mind is influenced to be accepting of others' viewpoints, but also is inquiring in forming opinions. There is great respect for justice and law. Jupiter is the natural Ruler of Sagittarius, so that the Jupiter qualities of expansion and good fortune should flow easily. The Sagittarian quality of optimism is most pronounced. There is an ability to overcome problems with trust that things will be better in the future. Since Sagittarius is the most active mental and physical Sign (in combination), this position increases the mental and physical activities.

### Capricorn

The Capricorn characteristics of ambition, conservation and responsibility are strongly emphasized when Jupiter is in this Sign. Willpower and self-control are very apparent. The mind is influenced to be practical, capable and serious. These people can be workaholics who really enjoy their work. The Capricorn quality of a slow, steady climb to the top is most pronounced. The career is usually with large corporations. Because of the cautious nature of Capricorn, the career is seldom a self-starting enterprise. There is a very strong sense of duty. The desire to conserve and be thrifty may appear as stinginess to others. There is a strict adherence to rules and regulations which can be extremely rigid. This placement enlarges the Capricorn seriousness, and there can be a lack of cheerfulness. Jupiter in Capricorn likes to amass wealth. When these thrifty people do spend money, they can be sponsors and patrons for different causes. The causes or events are usually of a practical nature.

## Aquarius

The Aquarian characteristics of humanitarianism, friendship and originality are expanded under Jupiter's influence. There is great enthusiasm for new ideas. The sociability of Jupiter bestows talent in working with groups. Since Aquarius is the most tolerant Sign, people with this placement are extremely tolerant and open to all types of people. They often enjoy groups of friends more than a close intimate relationship with only one person. This combination benefits the intellect, stimulating new, creative and imaginative concepts. There is often advanced ability in science, math or astrology. There is an interest in philosophical discussion, and a desire to help mankind. Jupiter usually brings added popularity to the well-liked Sign of Aquarius.

## Pisces

The Pisces qualities of sympathy, intuitive imagination and kindness are very apparent when Jupiter is in this Sign. The sensitive and impressionable characteristics of Pisces are accentuated. There is a wonderfully emotional response to the beauties of nature and the arts. This is the combination that often produces the Good Samaritan. These people are frequently found working in hospitals and public institutions. There are many doctors, nurses and people with religious vocations who have this placement. While these people are often quiet and unassuming, they usually have a delightful and subtle sense of humor. There is a capacity for pleasure that is often gently expressed. The Pisces dislike of confrontation is very pronounced. There is often a love of solitude. The quality of charity is strongly accented. The imagination is often gifted. Psychic ability can be enhanced. Spiritual and mystic tendencies are frequently in evidence.

# SATURN IN THE SIGNS
**Saturn is in each Sign approximately two to two and a half years.**

## Aries
Aries wants to get up and go. Saturn wants to stay and be cautious. So, Saturn in Aries causes tension and conflict. Strong desire to dominate others. In careers, there is often mechanical ability. Feelings of frustration from doing things at the wrong time. Strong willpower, self-reliance and endurance. Life often seems to be an obstacle course, but the ability is there to overcome. This position puts a damper on sociability, with a tendency to behave in a remote or aloof manner.

## Taurus
Taurean characteristics of perseverance, patience and stubbornness are pronounced. Saturn here tends to restrict the Taurus passion for beauty and luxury. The restrictive character usually inhibits and slows career success. Materialistic, so money and possessions are top priorities. Strong drive for security makes them careful with money, producing a strong desire to keep enlarging a savings account. Hard working, with a slow, steady climb to financial security. Very fixed thinking, with a lack of spontaneity and sense of compromise. Through being too cautious, they can miss opportunities. Dislike of public appearances.

## Gemini
Communication skills are inhibited and need cultivation. Bestows intellectual ability, with the thought process slow and deliberate. There is a lack of adaptability with an awkward and/or shy method of talking with others. On the plus side, Saturn gives structure to the flighty tendencies of Gemini. This combination often produces scholars. People with this placement can be serious and good teachers. There is frequently writing ability which focuses on important subjects. This produces strong critical ability. Travel is usually for business rather than pleasure. They can gradually develop an attractive speaking or writing style.

## Cancer
The emotions are often inhibited. There is an overwhelming concern for security. There is a tendency toward worry and melancholia,

with an overemphasis on the self. Restrictions are often felt because of family. Because of the emotional inhibitions, it is important that there is a good sexual relationship with the partner as an outlet for suppressed feelings. Strong tendency to hang on to old memories and souvenirs. They must guard against being too bossy. There is good business activity.

### Leo

Saturn in Leo gives strong willpower, organizational skills and self confidence. It inhibits the sense of fun. Restricts love relationships. Strong capacity for success in government and politics. Capable of leadership over large groups. Strongly disciplined, these people expect others to achieve the same way. They can become dictatorial. Their sense of nobility and dignity is strong, which sometimes makes them loners. At parties, they are usually discussing business or other serious subjects. Problems in love relationships if they keep too rigid an attitude.

### Virgo

Saturn here reinforces the Virgo characteristics of meticulous attention to detail, strong work instincts and critical ability. In work situations, there can be problems with people who work under them because they can be too critical of their work. There is also a tendency toward shyness. The mental ability is stable and practical. They have the capacity for long, hard work. They often work in isolation. There is great precision and clarity in writing. With Saturn, the career Planet, combined with Virgo, the Sign of work and service, these people would make ideal employees.

### Libra

Saturn functions well in Libra showing good judgment and a strong sense of responsiblity. Kindness is expressed. There can be problems in partnerships, however, through inhibition, which can lead to loneliness. Problems will involve the ability to compromise and share. Saturn here creates a fierce need to be accepted socially. Since the need for acceptance is so great, the Libra trait of insincerity must be guarded against. There is often success in the legal professions with this placement. If the career uses the artistic inclinations of Libra, it will be a no-nonsense approach to artistic matters. There will be good taste in clothing and art objects.

## Scorpio

The Scorpio characteristic of investigation and probing is intensified. Business ability is pronounced with an exacting attitude toward work. There is a very serious attitude toward life, with a tendency to brood. When Saturn combines with Scorpio, there can be a fierce drive for career success. With a strong penetrating mind, they can see through people immediately. They make very dangerous enemies. Saturn tries to restrain the emotional nature of Scorpio, so when this person finally lets go in anger, it can be like a volcano erupting. The negative qualities include stubbornness, jealousy and extreme secretiveness. Careers involving psychology or investigation are pronounced.

## Sagittarius

This placement produces responsible people who want to choose their own responsibilities. They are usually congenial people who like to mix business with pleasure. The interests of the higher mind are given great perseverance with this placement. There is pronounced involvement with religion, philosophy or the law. Saturn strengthens the mind. In Sagittarius, Saturn functions with more freedom. Saturn here restrains the extremes that Sagittarians like. It tends to produce balance and wisdom in the person. This combination usually shows good business success, making the person ambitious and able to work toward long range goals. There is a need to feel that they are always going forward, or frustrations can build up. Attracted to a serious, responsible partner who will not make emotional demands. They must guard against being too critical.

## Capricorn

Since Saturn rules Capricorn, this is its best placement. There is strong willpower, self-control, ambition, practical business ability and organizational skill. There are talents in diplomacy and economy of resources with an innate understanding of recycling. With a very responsible attitude toward work, there is slow, but sure, advancement. It sometimes takes these people a while to decide what they want to do in life. They need a career that stretches them. They usually reach full flower in middle age. Besides great organizing talent, this combination gives ability in handling the affairs of many departments or committees simultaneously. There is often writing talent.

### Aquarius

This placement usually produces an intuitive and finely developed mind. There can be mental obstinance. Saturn in Aquarius combines practicality with original thinking. There can be scientific ability and humanitarian instincts. While there may be desire for success, the planning for it is often not well thought out. Since Saturn is the career Planet, and Aquarius is a detached Air Sign, there can be indifference to career success. They can work in humanitarian fields without any need for recognition and public awareness of their success. There is often more emphasis put on groups of people rather than family relationships.

### Pisces

The rigidity of Saturn is softened in Pisces. It brings imagination and intuition to the mind. There can be sympathetic feelings toward others with a willingness for self-sacrifice. The problems that this placement brings are a feeling of hopelessness and a dependent attitude. This position calls for work to guard against loneliness and to develop a sense of hope. The career can be done in seclusion, without much recognition. There is usually great compassion for people in need, but often not toward their family. This combination gives an unusual mixture of good business ability and a lack of confidence. Also, the Pisces tendency toward self-sacrifice and the Saturn inclination to hold back and conserve are a difficult combination of extremes.

# URANUS IN THE SIGNS
## Uranus is in each Sign for approximately seven years.

### Aries
Uranus in Aries creates a strongly impulsive person. It strengthens the will and the ability to be independent. It adds great daring and courage to the leadership qualities. There can be sudden changes of energy or direction. This combination adds intellectual courage to the physical courage of Aries. There is ability to think quickly. To the pioneering instincts of Aries, Uranus adds the quality of revolution. These people make natural leaders, who usually are good troubleshooters. This is a placement of tremendous enthusiasm. It is also a very impatient placement, requiring the need to develop caution.

### Taurus
This combination creates a fixed, stubborn, immovable mind. It increases determination. There is an interesting combination of the Uranus desire for the new and unusual, mixed with the Taurus desire for money and possessions. So, they can be attracted to different ways of earning money and they can have a desire for new and/or unusual collectibles. Since Uranus is sudden and erratic, there could be a sudden windfall, or a sudden loss of money. There can be drastic changes in self-earned income. This placement makes the stubbornness of Taurus even more pronounced, but Taurus helps stabilize the erratic nature of Uranus. Among the pluses is the ability to function well working as part of a team, and being farsighted in practical, artistic matters.

### Gemini
This placement adds ingenuity and inventiveness to the mind. There can be original writing talent. The mind is quick. There is often talent with electronics, especially computers. The Gemini characteristic of liking lots of activity is accentuated. The Gemini interest in communication is usually strongly emphasized — with a love of talking on the phone, reading and often writing. The tremendous energy of Uranus added to the very active Sign of Gemini can produce nervous, easily irritated people. There can be frequent changes in jobs until the right career is found.

## Cancer

With Uranus in Cancer there is usually a pronounced interest in the new and unusual in the home, while still having an attachment for the past. The imagination and the instincts are strengthened and stimulated. There is a need to be cautious about getting upset over too many little things. Patriotic feelings are increased. The urge to break away from family and home can be pronounced. Uranus here adds an unpredictable quality to the character.

## Leo

Uranus in Leo awakens the willpower. There is often pronounced leadership ability, but it will be unusual in some way. The Fifth House areas of pleasure and drama are strongly emphasized. There is ability to harness and focus complete energy on whatever is at hand. There can be a strong desire to speculate or gamble. The desire for leadership can be so strong that this person can be involved in power struggles. If there is creativity shown in the Chart, this placement will add originality to it.

## Virgo

Uranus in Virgo generally awakens the interest in a clean environment. The analytical ability of Virgo is strengthened and there is often pronounced ability to think of problem solving ideas in work situations. Interest in new and innovative ideas about health and hygiene is apparent. The powers of discrimination can be so pronounced that these people are often too critical. They can become dogmatic. Unless sensitivity is emphasized elsewhere in the Chart, they can be too detached and lacking in feelings for others. This can create problems in working with others.

## Libra

With Uranus in Libra there is an interest and appreciation of trends in the arts. There is frequently artistic talent. Since Libra is the Sign of partnership, Uranus here brings about unusual attitudes in partnerships. There can be a sense of compromise toward the partner. There can also be a sudden change in partners. People with this placement will be interested in new ideas about justice. They can have innovative ideas about the law. Since Libra is the public relations Sign, Uranus will add intuitive thinking in this area.

## Scorpio

Uranus emphasizes the Scorpio intensity. There is ability in investigation. The strong Scorpio willpower becomes even stronger through Uranus' influence. There is great drive and perseverance. With fierce powers of concentration, they can do innovative work in scientific or psychological fields. Uranus in Scorpio produces a very stubborn individual. All this power can be used for good or evil.

## Sagittarius

In Sagittarius, Uranus stimulates new concepts in the Ninth House subjects of philosophy, religion and higher education. Uranus emphasizes the Sagittarian love of freedom to an even greater degree. This combination often produces a person who is high spirited and likes to be on the move. This is not a placement that naturally inclines toward marriage. The Aquarian/Uranian interest in astrology is frequently reflected in the religious thinking of these people. There is often a wish to reform religious thinking.

## Capricorn

Uranus brings to the practical Earth Sign of Capricorn the ability to be flexible. It often brings brilliant ideas to the mind which can be used in business. Since Capricorn is the career Sign, Uranus gives it even stronger ambitions for success. There is often ability in handling finances and a knack for recognizing opportunities. Perseverance is very pronounced. In fact, these people can be so intent on work that they may neglect their social contacts. Strong organizational skills are evident. They make hard working, fair employers.

## Aquarius

In Aquarius, Uranus is in its own Sign. This is the position of the progressive thinker. These people have ideas that are way ahead of their time. They possess originality. The Aquarian quality of detachment is quite pronounced, but there is great interest in humanitarian projects. Uranus in this Sign strengthens the will. It also intensifies the fixed quality of Aquarius, making the person seem to enjoy taking the opposite point of view and standing firm. This combination produces the revolutionary whose ideas are often not appreciated until it's after the fact.

**Pisces**

There is an intuitive mind with this combination. The imagination is strong and vivid, with ideas coming in flashes. There is an inclination toward spiritual values. The ability for self-sacrifice exists. The problems that can occur with this placement are a tendency to daydream and not put the good ideas to use. There can also be a desire for an escape mechanism when the pressure gets too strong. With the Uranus quality of humanitarianism added to Pisces (the most sympathetic Sign), there is concern for the welfare of mankind.

Note: Due to apprent retrograde motion, some Planets move into a new Sign one year, and then appear to move back into the previous Sign for a short itme. So the years of change from one Sign to another can overlap.

# NEPTUNE IN THE SIGNS

**Neptune is in each Sign from twelve to fifteen years. It takes approximately 164 years to complete its orbit around the Sun.**

## Aries

(1861 to 1875)

Neptune is less passive in this Sign. There can be radical ideas and an unselfish attitude in trying to realize goals. There is often interest in promoting spiritual matters. With Neptune in Aries, there can be confusion and illusion involving wars. True photography was invented when Neptune (the Planet of illusion) was in the inventive Sign of Aquarius. It flowered when Neptune was in Pisces. When Neptune Transited the Sign of Aries, there were significant breakthroughs in film, particularly in 1871. Aries is a Sign of original thinking and pioneering.

## Taurus

(1874 to 1888)

Since Taurus is ruled by Venus, which makes the Sign responsive to beauty, Neptune here increases the attraction to art and good design. Neptune also inclines people to search for perfection in law. This idealism is also carried into the financial realm of Taurus-related matters.

## Gemini

(1888 to 1902)

Neptune brings the intuitive imagination into the field of communication and writing. It enhances sensitivity. There are powers of persuasion in communicating. There can be a lack of practical thinking, with a tendency to worry.

## Cancer

(1901 - 1915)

Neptune intensifies the emotional and sensitive ties to the family and home in Cancer. There are often psychic and instinctive responses to daily living. Ties to religion are usually emotional. Patriotism is pronounced. This is an affectionate influence.

## Leo

(1914 - 1929)

The Planet of the imagination in the most creative Sign combines strong leadership ability in the field of the arts, especially the cinema. The movies came into being when Neptune was in Leo from 1914 to 1929. On a personal basis, there can be illusion as to one's own artistic ability and organizational skills. This is especially pronounced when Neptune is in the First House with Leo on the Ascendant. Neptune in Leo had a dramatic impact on art. The great modern artists of this period include Matisse, Chagall, Miro, Modigliani and Picasso.

## Virgo

(1928 - 1943)

This was a period of the idealization of the worker. Labor unions were formed during this time. Abstract ideas were brought into practical reality. There was great interest in health and hygiene. The study of psychosomatic illness came into practice. There was an interest in the area of healing. Films during this period often focused on the common man.

## Libra

(1943 - 1957)

Neptune brought idealism into relationships in Libra. There is a longing for soul mate. This period produced the flower children. There is an attraction to the easy life with little emphasis on material goods. There is also an interest in drugs. In contrast to Neptune in practical Virgo, Neptune in Libra produced impractical idealism. There is a tendency toward platonic love of the community. There is a wish for justice and the ability to compromise.

## Scorpio

(1957 - 1970)

The combination of Neptune in Scorpio creates a strong desire for any kind of sensation. This was a period of excess with drugs, alcohol and crime. Since Scorpio is the Sign of sex, and Neptune represents drugs, this was the era that developed the pill to prevent pregnancies. This period also marked drastic changes in censorship. Movies and television (also ruled by Neptune) became open and graphic in regard to sex. There was a fascination with things that used to be hidden. Instinctive intuition is heightened. Since Neptune represents illusion and confusion, and Scorpio relates to sex, this was a time of unisex influence in dress. Women, en masse, began wearing pants everywhere. Men began wearing long hair and more feminine clothing.

## Sagittarius
(1970 - 1984)

The psychic influence of Neptune was felt in the Sagittarian realm of higher education. There was a longing for higher knowledge and an interest in astrology and psychic phenomena. Since Neptune dissolves things, the rigidity of religious belief was broken down. But while Sagittarius loves freedom, it is the Sign of law, so there was a dissolution of fixed religious beliefs, but there was still a respect for religion. There was a greater freedom in exploring philosophic ideas. The optimistic influence of Sagittarius was felt in this generation of people. They have the power to visualize. If Neptune is well Aspected in a Natal Chart, and is placed in (or strongly influencing) the Ninth or Tenth House, there should be the talent of the good philosopher. Universities during this period became less materialistic.

## Capricorn
(1984 - 1998)

This is the period when the abstract thinking, developed when Neptune was in Sagittarius, can be given structure and form in Capricorn. The idealism which promoted the ideas in Sagittarius will be utilized for practical purposes in Capricorn. Not all of the goals will be realized, because Neptune seeks the ideal, which is not always obtainable. Under Capricorn's influence, this ideal can become practical and traditional in concept. Ambition and drive for success can be watered down by Neptune. Neptune is also the Planet of the musician. The recording industry's Grammy Awards for 1987 are referred to as "the year of the dinosaur." There were more musicians and singers who received nominations and awards from an older age group than ever before in the history of the Grammys. Capricorn represents old age. With Neptune, which rules cinema, in Capricorn, there is an emphasis on older actors in film and television. This is already apparent. When Neptune was last in

Capricorn, in the early 19th century, the comic opera "The Barber of Seville" by Rossini was first introduced. This opera became the model for all the later writers of comic opera. This opera form combined the Neptune/music influence with the Capricorn wit.

## Aquarius

(1997 - 2011)

There will be an idealistic approach to humanitarian concerns. The intuitive creativity of Neptune combined with the inventive, original thinking of Aquarius should produce many new breakthroughs in science and technology. Inventions should benefit mankind. Because of the creative capacity of Neptune, and the Aquarian drive for the new and unusual, new art forms will emerge. Intuitive and psychic thinking can become pronounced during this period. Neptune is the Planet of illusion, and Aquarius is the Sign of the inventor and scientist. During the last Transit of Neptune through Aquarius (1834 - 1847), true photography, which was first developed in 1826, flourished. Great improvements were made in 1840 and 1841.

## Pisces

(2011)

Neptune in Pisces will bring about a peaceful period. Neptune is the ruler of Pisces and functions best in this Sign. It stimulates the spiritual, intuitive side of mankind. Mystical ideas will be at the forefront. There will be ability to understand and help the suffering of mankind. This combination of Planet and Sign puts a damper on dynamic action. However, there should be a flowering of art, music and cinema. When Neptune was last in Pisces (1847 - 1862), it marked the period of the great French Impressionist painters. Since Pisces is the most impressionable Sign, and Neptune is the Planet of the imagination, this is a perfect example of a Planet functioning in a Sign. True photography, which was invented during Neptune's Transit of Aquarius, flowered while Neptune was in Pisces. The ancient Greeks had developed the "camera obscura" which was a simple pinhole camera with a translucent screen. Two important photographic processes were developed in 1850 and 1851. Since Neptune is the musician's Planet, and Pisces is the Sign of artists and musicians, there was a flowering of music when Neptune was in its own Sign of Pisces. Some of the gifted composers of this time were Verdi, Bizet, Gounod, Offenbach and Wagner. Rossini also continued composing during this period.

# PLUTO IN THE SIGNS

**Pluto has an irregular orbit and stays in a Sign between 12 to 30 years. Since it is so slow moving, it brings a generational influence.**

## Aries

(1823 - 1851)

Pluto has the greatest energy in Aries. It awakens the pioneering instincts. During this period, the exploration of the West occurred in America. In Europe, people fought for liberty and freedom from monarchies. There is tremendous drive and great strength of will. A desire for adventure is pronounced. There is a will to fight for new ideas and reform. The courage and strength to overcome difficulties is at its strongest.

## Taurus

(1851-52 - 1883 - 84)

Taurus has a quality of great perseverance which is strengthened by Pluto. This combination stabilized the changes brought by Pluto in Aries. The Taurus characteristic of drive for wealth was most pronounced during this period. The desire for land was also at the forefront. Business and industry were expanded and standardized. Structure was developed in corporations. There was a great divergence in the classes of people caused by wealth on one end to poverty at the other.

## Gemini

(1883-84 - 1912-13)

Since Gemini rules the Third House of communication and the immediate environment, great changes took place in these areas. The automobile and the airplane were invented. Thomas Edison invented the light bulb and the phonograph. Alexander Graham Bell invented the telephone. Mass production was developed in many industries. Gemini is a clever, inventive Sign, and Pluto took that power to the heights. Gemini also rules lower education, and this was the period when compulsory education began.

## Cancer

(1913-14 - 1937-38)

Pluto strongly affected the Cancer-ruled areas of family, home and food. It was the period of World War I and the Great Depression. Families were uprooted. Women began working outside the home, as they became emancipated and were granted the right to vote. For the first time in American history, a woman was appointed as a Presidential Cabinet member. Patriotism, which is a natural quality of Cancer, was most pronounced. Cancer is also the most tenacious Sign, and there was struggle and strength to find security.

## Leo

(1937-38 - 1957)

The Leo qualities of willpower, pride, drama and self-confidence became powerfully evident. Since Leo is a creative Sign and Pluto represents power, this was the period when atomic energy was discovered. It was the era of dictators and World War II. People born during this period like to be in positions of authority, and usually possess a lot of self-confidence. Pluto strengthened the natural creativity of Leo.

## Virgo

(1957 - 1972)

Virgo is an analytical, orderly Sign. With Pluto in Virgo, the ability to use knowledge in practical ways was heightened. This was the birth period for the electronics and computer industries. Automation was introduced in manufacturing. There was pronounced interest in health and hygiene, with a desire for higher standards in these areas. The birth control pill was developed. This was a period of striving for perfection in the Virgo areas of work, service and health. Natural foods became popular.

## Libra

(1972 - 1984)

With Libra as the Sign of justice, there was great concern for social justice when Pluto was in this Sign. There was also interest in prison reform. With Pluto, the Planet of death and rebirth in Libra, the Supreme

Court ruled on 6/29/72 that capital punishment was in violation of the Constitution because it was cruel and unusual punishment since it was arbitrary and discriminatory.  There was a rebirth in ths law on 7/2/76 when the Supreme Court ruled that it was not cruel and unusual punishment inherently, but banned "mandatory" capital punishment.  It ruled that the judge and jury must be given adequate information and guidance.  As Libra is also the Sign of partnership and marriage, Pluto brought about great changes in these areas.  There was a strong desire for peace, but many disruptions threatened peace.  The Libra love of art and beauty was also most pronounced.

## Scorpio
### (1984 - 1995)

Since Pluto represents the underworld, and Scorpio is the most intense, secretive Sign, this is the period of terrorism.  In this very emotional Sign, Pluto will bring the power of resistance.  It also increases the penetrating skills of Scorpio.  Since Pluto rules Scorpio, it will have its greatest strength here.  Scorpio has the widest swing between good and evil.  Scorpio rules insurance and taxes.  There should be sweeping changes in these areas during this period.  While this can be a time of destruction, the desire and power for regeneration will be there.  Pluto also rules the sex organs, and Scorpio rules the Eighth House of sexuality.
The AIDS disease is becoming widespread.  Pluto is causing death from a sexually communicated illness.  But it will also bring about a rebirth and regeneration.

## Sagittarius
### (1995 - 2009)

Pluto in Sagittarius will bring power to the areas of higher education and abstract thinking.  It will also strongly affect religion and law.  Pluto will change these areas through transformation and regeneration.  There will be enthusiasm for truth.  When Pluto was last in Sagittarius from 1749 to 1762, the first encyclopedia was published.  Sagittarius also represents publishing, so the encyclopedia involved three Sagittarian areas — the higher mind, truth, and publishing.  Since Sagittarius is the Sign of distant travel, this will be a period of great development in this area.

## Capricorn

(2008 - 2024)

Since Capricorn is the Sign of career and business, Pluto will bring about changes in these areas. There will be a great desire for recognition and success. There will be tremendous emphasis on organization and regulation. The political qualities of Capricorn will be pronounced. When Pluto was last in Capricorn (from 1762 to 1777), it was the period of the Industrial Revolution. Rules and regulations were set down by the American Congress for the new nation of the United States during this period.

## Aquarius

(2024 - 2050)

With the Aquarian need for freedom, when Pluto was last in this Sign (1777 to 1798), it marked the period of the American and French Revolutions. This combination produces a deep basic drive for freedom. Aquarius is also the Sign of humanitarianism and the group instinct. It should be a period of great regeneration in these areas in the 21st century. Aquarius is the Sign of the inventor, the scientist and the astrologer, so there could be progress in these separate fields.

## Pisces

(2050)

Pisces represents intuitive creativity. When it is combined with Pluto, it can produce sensitivity and imaginative growth in the arts. When Pluto was last in Pisces (1798 to 1823), it marked the Romantic Period in the areas of art, music and literature. Pisces also represents the unconscious, and mystical parts of our nature. Pluto stimulates our feelings of sympathy and compassion. It also influences our willingness toward self-sacrifice.

# THE SUN THROUGH THE HOUSES

First
* Strong body and personality
* Willpower
* Drive for prominence
* Vitality
* Dignity
* Strong self image

Second
* Drive for prominence
* Love of beautiful possessions
* Generous
* Materialistic outlook
* Great importance placed on security

Third
* Communication skills
* Pleasant, lively conversationalist
* Enjoys siblings and neighbors
* Loves to travel around town
* Likes to spread information

Fourth
* Your home is your castle
* Talent for products of the home, food, and real estate
* Family life is very important
* Possible career from home

Fifth
* Ability in the creative fields and games, including sports
* Love and romance are of great importance
* Pleasure-seeker
* Self-confidence

* Leadership ability

Sixth

* Your work is everything to you
* Drive for doing a job well
* Ability in health-related fields
* Service oriented
* Analytical, critical talent
* Good health, unless Sun has several hard Aspects to it

Seventh

* Marriage and/or partnerships are the center of your universe
* Desire for important relationships
* Drive for prominence

Eighth

* Interest in the unknown
* Talent for investigation
* Willpower
* Passionate

Ninth

* Strong, abstract mind
* Desire for wisdom and understanding
* Love of travel and foreign lands
* Success comes through study
* High ideals

Tenth

* Strong drive for career
* Major thrust is financial and public success
* Personal magnetism
* Very ambitious
* Drive for prominent position

Eleventh

* Popular position

* Benefits through friends
* Leadership ability with groups and organizations
* Wishing for success, rather than striving for it
* Co-operation
* Sociable
* Able to achieve on your own

Twelfth

* Love of seclusion
* Needs to find area of dedication and service
* Able to sacrifice
* Problems with real self-expression

# THE MOON THROUGH THE HOUSES

First

* Sensitive
* Emotional nature
* Fluctuating energy and moods
* Very impressionable
* Lack of long-range planning
* Need for recognition

Second

* Money comes and goes quickly
* Need for financial security
* Business ability in career-ruled matters of the home, food, or real estate
* Enjoy spending money on family and home

Third

* Common sense
* Logical thought is affected by emotions and imagination
* Benefits memory
* Active imagination
* Thinking is absorbed with mundane matters
* Restless

Fourth

* Parents are very important to you
* Emotionally attached to your home
* Many changes of residence, or changes within the home, especially in early years
* Intuitive
* Possible public recognition
* Often fond of domestic chores
* Business often involves Fourth House matters of home, food, or real estate

Fifth

* Love affairs, with strongly romantic feelings
* Pleasure seeker, with changes of interest in types of pleasure
* In a man's Chart it indicates strong affection for his mother
* Fertile position for women, especially in a Water Sign
* Emotional enjoyment of children

Sixth

* Frequent, minor health problems
* Inclined to serve
* Work fluctuates according to moods
* Usually likes small pets
* Possible frequent changes of job

Seventh

* Opportunities to marry
* Emotional need for marriage and home
* Relationships with women are important
* Need for emotional rapport with partner
* Tendency to marry for security
* Good business sense

Eighth

* Good placement for psychic research
* Sensitivity to death and after-life
* Possible inheritance from mother, or wife, or family
* Strong psychic sensitivity
* Fluctuations with partner's finances

Ninth

* Teaching ability
* Ability to study serious subjects
* Fertile imagination
* Emotionally attached to religious and ethical beliefs from upbringing
* Intuitive and/or psychic

* Possible inspired, intuitive thinking
* Emotionally attracted to foreign lands

Tenth

* Desire for public recognition
* Working with the public
* Possible changes in career interests
* Career benefits through women
* Natural rapport with people

Eleventh

* Popularity
* Good social ability
* Emotional need for friends and groups
* Often join groups related to home interests
* Women friends, more than men friends

Twelfth

* Need for seclusion to recharge batteries
* Intuitive, psychic
* Extremely emotionally sensitive
* Very imaginative
* Moods affected by the subconscious mind
* Inhibits emotional expression

# MERCURY THROUGH THE HOUSES

First

* Mentally alert and active
* Talkative
* Nervous
* Quick in speech and writing
* Can be too self-absorbed

Second

* Financial ability
* Able to make money through writing and speaking
* Mind focuses on money and possessions
* Often indicates sales ability

Third

* Studious
* Verbal skills
* Teaching ability
* Possible writing talent
* Curious active mind
* Talkative

Fourth

* Highstrung
* Tendency to change homes
* At home with many books, or studies at home
* Rational attitude toward home and family

Fifth

* Creative writing and speaking ability
* Enjoyment of intellectual games
* Romantic affairs of the mind
* Easy communication with children and young people

Sixth

* Talking is connected to work
* Specialized knowledge or skill
* Tends to be concerned about health
* Interest in hygiene
* Practical thinking related to job

Seventh

* Attracted to intellectual partner
* You like to think in partnership
* Wants lively, stiumlating communication
* Needs marriage that is active and adaptable, with a clever, interesting partner
* Often interested in psychology

Eighth

* Ability for in-depth research
* Strengthens mental ability
* Interest in Eighth House matters including taxes, insurance, corporate finances, business or money connected with death; the occult
* Enjoyment of mystery stories
* Often indicates a penetrating mind

Ninth

* Mental ability in abstract thought
* Possible careers in teaching, writing, or travel
* Desire for long-distance travel
* Often talent with foreign languages
* Strong, and often broad, mental interest in Ninth House matters —law, philosophy, higher education, and/or foreign lands
* Higher education is important to you

Tenth

* Likes business conversation
* Communication plays significant role in your career; skill in this area, unless Mercury is intercepted

* Need for intellectually stimulating career
* Good position for commercial or literary success
* Change of careers, possibly two careers simultaneously
* Ambition, with organization and planning ability
* Recognition comes from mental activity
* Indicates quick, outgoing mental energy

Eleventh
* Communication with friends
* Wants lively, intellectual friends
* Possible spokesperson for groups
* Interest in new ideas and inventions
* Enjoys wide circle of friends
* Ability to talk with people from all walks of life
* Possible career benefits through friends

Twelfth
* Intuitive mind
* Often secretive
* Hinders verbal and writing communication unless Conjunct the Ascendant
* Active imagination
* Prefers to work in seclusion

# VENUS THROUGH THE HOUSES

First
* Usually bestows good looks
* Interest in dressing well and looking good
* Attuned to the arts
* Pleasant, social

Second
* Love of beautiful possessions
* Lucky with finances
* Money spent on (and often earned through) decorative and ornamental things

Third
* Pleasant manner of speaking
* The mundane mind is bright in creative and artistic areas
* Dislike of confrontation
* Interesting and charming conversationalist
* Ability to express love

Fourth
* Love of home
* Desire for attractive surroundings
* Needs harmony at home
* Often come from an attractive or cultured home
* A truly loving person with a strong affection for the parents, especially the mother

Fifth
* Love of creativity
* Affectionate with loved one and children
* The thrill of romance
* Love of spotlight
* Pleasant and/or attractive children
* Enjoyment of games and sports

Sixth

* Dedicated to work
* Congenial relationship with employers and co-workers
* Work is often related to artistic fields
* Love has a practical influence here
* Health problems may involve throat, kidneys, or generative organs

Seventh

* Attracted to a good-looking partner
* Often indicates a fortunate marriage
* Enjoyment of close personal relationships
* If Venus is well Aspected here, there can be successful business partnerships
* Social, affectionate

Eighth

* Attractive sexuality
* Physical expression of love
* Financial benefits from partner
* Possible inheritance
* Peaceful death

Ninth

* Love of Ninth House subjects — travel, abstract thought, philosophy, and books
* Enjoyment of higher education
* Easy sociability with foreigners
* Creative higher mind
* Idealistic love nature

Tenth

* Career usually focuses on artistic subjects
* Often brings success to your career
* Smooth, diplomatic public manner
* Makes you attractive to the public
* Satisfaction and pleasure from career

Eleventh

* Friends bring you pleasure and happiness
* Venus here usually makes you popular
* Success with groups and clubs
* Attracted to new art forms and/or artistic friends
* In a man's Chart, women friends are attracted to you

Twelfth

* Love of mystic and/or occult subjects
* Unselfish
* Possible secret love affairs
* Enjoyment of seclusion
* Pleasure in music and art

# MARS THROUGH THE HOUSES

First
* Very energetic
* Strong passions
* Assertive
* Courageous
* Enjoys strenuous activities
* Competitive
* Impatient and impulsive

Second
* Ambitious
* Energy is put into earning money
* Money can be earned quickly and is usually quickly spent
* Ability to earn money can be through Mars-related fields
* Sales ability
* Strong capacity for work

Third
* Energized communication
* Very active and aggressive in short trips about town
* The mind is alert, enthusiastic, and independent
* Verbally agressive — likes to argue
* Quick-witted
* Wants to be first at everything

Fourth
* Energy is put into the home
* Inherits strong constitution
* Your childhood home was a very busy, active place
* Need for energy outlet through work involving home or home-related products

Fifth
* Creative drive
* Excellent placement for athletic competition
* Strong passion in love affairs

* Active children
* Enjoys participating in, or watching, athletic events
* Self confident

Sixth

* Hard worker
* Automatically pitches in where needed
* Efficient
* Effective sales ability
* Good vitality
* Ability to use situations to your advantage
* Conscientious

Seventh

* This placement attracts a strong, aggressive partner
* The marriage may involve many arguments
* Drive for teamwork
* A lively, active marriage

Eighth

* Ability in research
* Strong self drive
* Drive for power
* Involvement with other people's money
* Instinct for survival
* Death will be quite often accidental

Ninth

* Enthusiastic love of intellectual learning
* Good placement for a career in travel
* Independent thinker
* Likes the activity of travel
* Enjoyment and talent in outdoor sports
* Desire to persuade others to your point of view

Tenth

* Tremendous career drive and energy

* Independent
* Very active career
* Drive for success
* Ambition to reach the top in your profession

Eleventh
* Energy is directed towards friends and groups
* Socially popular — usually a leader in your circle of friends
* Attracts new friends
* Enjoys sports activities with friends
* Helpful to friends

Twelfth
* Your real drive is hidden from view
* Able to turn things to your advantage
* Aggressive energy is turned inward which can cause health problems
* Interested in swords and knives
* Impatient
* Deeply secretive

# JUPITER THROUGH THE HOUSES

**First**

* Cheerful
* Generous
* Love of travel
* Need for freedom
* Often lucky or fortunate

**Second**

* An excellent placement for making money
* Good fortune in financial matters
* Money making talent is often connected with Ninth House matters — law, publishing, travel, or religion

**Third**

* Enjoys communicating and sharing ideas
* Likes school
* Teaching ability
* Very "talky" — likes to use a lot of words

**Fourth**

* Usually indicates happy relationship with parents
* Growing up in a comfortable home
* Business benefits would come through real estate, home products or design, or the food business

**Fifth**

* Love of pleasure and games
* Ability in sports
* Indicative of happiness through large family
* Increases creative talent

**Sixth**

* Good health when not overindulgent
* Need for independence in work
* Likes to serve

* A job with lots of mobility is best

Seventh
* Benefits marriage and partnerships
* Financial and social gains through marriage
* Usually makes social contacts and conversation easy
* The Aspects to Jupiter will indicate how successful it works here
* Indicates success with lawsuits

Eighth
* Money benefits from partner
* Large appetite for sex
* A confident, optimistic attitude toward life
* Good placement for inheritance
* No fear of death
* A peaceful death from natural causes

Ninth
* Superb placement for Jupiter
* Strong benefits to the higher mind
* Profound interest in philosophy, religion, law, morality and ethics
* Successful position for publishing and long distance travel
* A cheerful, optimistic outlook

Tenth
* Great benefits to the career
* This position indicates public honor and recognition
* Strong leadership ability
* Career will benefit from Ninth House connection — law, philosophy, travel, publishing, etc.

Eleventh
* Terrific location for popularity
* Large circle of friends

* Benefits from friends and groups
* Financial success through career
* Interest in humanitarian causes

Twelfth
* Interest in mysticism and religion
* Psychic ability
* Adversity turns into success
* Enjoyment of seclusion
* Good placement for work in medicine and intellectual careers

## SATURN THROUGH THE HOUSES

First

* Serious
* Responsible
* Conservative appearance
* Ambitious, career minded
* Self-controlled
* Selfish
* Hard working
* Inhibited personality lacking real self-confidence
* Born "old" — you get younger as you age

Second

* Cautious with money, thrifty
* Money comes in very slowly through your own career or efforts
* Must work hard for what you earn
* Financial success can come after years of striving
* Problems or worries with finances
* Often very "tight" with your money

Third

* Restricts communication or makes it precise
* The mind is serious, cautious, slow in coming into full power
* Had to work hard in school to succeed
* Logical mind
* Heavy responsibility with siblings, or neighbors, or communication
* Slow, cautious drive
* Often late for appointments

Fourth

* Difficult family life as a child
* Father either a problem or absent from home
* Stern parents with strict ideas of right and wrong

* Restricted or lonely circumstances at end of life
* Feelings of insecurity

## Fifth

* Approach to pleasure is very serious
* This placement restricts offspring, or causes problems with them
* Inhibits creative talent
* Attracted to older, or serious person in love relationship
* Relaxation is difficult
* Subdues love nature

## Sixth

* Reliable, hard worker
* Serious, systematic approach to work
* Health problems from slow recuperation to problems with teeth and bones
* Great attention to accuracy and details in work

## Seventh

* Either a late marriage or a very long lasting one
* Serious, responsible attitude toward partner
* You will have to work hard in support of your marriage or partnership
* A sense of duty toward partner

## Eighth

* Inhibits sexual expression
* Responsible attitude in handling other people's money, including partners
* Self-disciplined
* Serious attitude toward life, death and sex
* Indicates death in old age
* Money can come from property

Ninth

* Inhibits enthusiasm
* The higher mind is serious, with the ability to concentrate, but must guard against overwork
* Problems with travel, or travel will not be for pleasure, but part of your career
* Career often involves Ninth House matters of religion, law, philosophy, or publishing

Tenth

* This is Saturn's natural home, so it functions well here.
* Success in career due to responsibility, talent, and hard work
* Ambitious
* Slow, steady climb to the top
* Desire for recognition
* Gives business ability

Eleventh

* Financial success in career will be earned the hard way — through long steady application
* Highly selective of friends, preferring a limited number of serious, reliable friends who become life-long supportive friends
* Usually takes on heavy responsibilities in groups and or- ganizations as a leader

Twelfth

* Saturn here usually indicates a career in seclusion
* Serious attitude toward psychic and mystic matters
* Extreme sensitivity
* Ability and preference for working alone
* A tendency to keep problems to yourself
* Often inhibits recognition in career

## URANUS THROUGH THE HOUSES

First
* Extremely independent and original
* Magnetic personality
* Lively, active
* Highstrung
* Lightning-like responses and comprehension
* Energy comes in sudden spurts
* Idealistic
* Intense need for freedom
* A leader, rather than a follower
* Creative

Second
* Money earned through unusual occupations
* Sudden changes in income
* Clever problem solving
* Best suited to your own business which you can create
* Income is seldom from time-clock punching, steady career
* Money can suddenly come from commissions or completions of job projects

Third
* Original style of writing and communicating
* Distinctive speaking voice
* Quick comprehension
* Lower education will be lively
* Active
* Independent

Fourth
* Unusual home life
* Often seeks freedom from home
* Likes unusual people
* There can be many changes in the home environment

Fifth
* Different, out-of-the-ordinary recreation
* Sudden, powerful attractions in love relationships
* Likes exciting entertainment
* Children are often gifted
* Creativity is distinctly original

Sixth
* Work usually involves electronics, computers, scientific areas or astrology
* Work has an unusual element like great freedom or originality
* Health can benefit from unusual methods of treatment

Seventh
* Unusual or different marriage and/or partnership
* Partner will be a unique person
* Independent and romantic attitude toward partner
* Sudden attractions
* Relationships can be erratic

Eighth
* Interest in astrology, life after death, and the unknown
* Unusual attitude or ideas about sex
* Possible unexpected money comes to you from unusual sources

Ninth
* Exciting long distance travel
* Trips can be sudden and unexpected
* Creative, independent higher mind
* Often interested in science or metaphysics
* Unconventional attitude
* Possibility of being accident prone

Tenth
* Technical ability
* New inventions often benefit career through your ability to utilize new products and ideas
* Adapts easily to changes in career
* A dislike of routine — job should be lively

Eleventh
* Unusual friends
* Enjoyment of friends and groups
* Changes in friendships
* Progressive ideals and goals

Twelfth
* Psychic ability is unusual
* Highly intuitive
* Attracted to mysticism and secrets

# NEPTUNE THROUGH THE HOUSES

First
* Extremely sensitive and intuitive
* Vulnerable, impressionable
* Imaginative, artistic
* Idealistic
* Neptune here can weaken the personality or incline to laziness unless strongly Aspected
* Sensitivity to drugs and alcohol

Second
* Lack of clear vision with involved finances
* A vague attitude toward money
* There can be financial problems including deception from others
* Money often made from use of your imagination or intuition
* Too generous with money
* Strong desire to own beautiful objects
* Enjoys alcohol or nicotine

Third
* Intuitive mind
* Very emotional
* Good speaking ability
* Imaginative
* Impressionable
* Sensitivity in understanding others
* Strong powers of visualization
* Interest in mystical and occult studies — often writing about these subjects

Fourth
* Idealistic about home and family
* An artistic or psychic parent
* A sensitive, affectionate nature
* A tendency toward melancholy

  * There can be mysteries or secrets involving the family
  * The end of life can be spent in contemplation, seclusion or meditation

Fifth

  * Enjoyment of artistic entertainment, especially music, films and theater
  * Tendency to see children and spouse through rose colored glasses
  * Acting ability
  * Confusion in love affairs
  * Love of romance
  * Often produces sensitive, spiritual children

Sixth

  * A tendency toward laziness in work
  * Inclined to artistic work or helping the needy
  * Interest in the art of healing, often working in hospitals
  * Problems with medications and drugs
  * Imbalance in body chemistry
  * Possible problems with co-workers
  * A desire to care for pets

Seventh

  * Desire for perfect marriage, looking for soul mate
  * Possible spiritual or platonic marriage
  * Partner could be nebulous or alcoholic
  * Self-sacrificing attitude toward partner
  * Partner could be religious or artistic
  * Psychic or karmic connection with partner
  * Receptive to others
  * Artistic ability and/or appreciation

Eighth

  * Very sensual sexuality

* Possible disillusion with money from others
* Need for financial advice
* Sensitive, psychic
* Problems with drugs
* Strong senses and instincts
* Periods of depression
* Interest in occult matters

Ninth

* Desire for higher education involving the arts
* Idealistic
* Active, impressionable mind
* Interest in mystical types of religion
* Intuitive and/or psychic mind
* Strong imagination which can be over-active

Tenth

* Career in the arts, religion, psychology, or astrology
* Often gives magnetic appeal to the public
* This shows career drive, but makes you desire high goals
* There can be different directions in careers
* Possible lack of honesty if negatively Aspected

Eleventh

* Attracted to mystical or artistic friends
* Can be easily influenced by friends, unless strongly Aspected
* Secretive friendships
* Easily tempted by friends if weakly Aspected
* Idealistic attitude toward friends
* Desire to belong to religions or humanitarian groups and or-
  ganizations

Twelfth

* Attracted to contemplative life
* Spiritual depth from the past
* Possible drug or alcohol addiction
* Interest in charitable organizations

* Strong creative influence
* This is a very compassionate placement when well Aspected

# PLUTO THROUGH THE HOUSES

First
* Magnetic personality
* This placement gives great potential, especially if strongly Aspected
* Powerful person
* When Pluto is close to the Ascendant, it adds strong sexuality to the appearance

Second
* Powerful ability to earn money
* Money is a driving force in life
* There can be financial extremes
* The desire to obtain possessions

Third
* Vital need for communication
* Great interest in siblings and neighbors
* Gives depth and strength to the mind
* Good powers of concentration, unless negatively Aspected
* A penetrating, probing mind
* Powerful ability to influence others' thinking

Fourth
* Powerful attachment to your home
* Strong parental influence
* Intensifies feelings in family situations, which need discipline for happy domestic life
* Childhood can have difficulties because of parental upsets
* There is usually isolation at the end of life
* An inclination toward contemplation

Fifth
* Vital need for creative expression

* Love affairs will be passionate and powerful
* Impetuous attitude toward Fifth House matters
* Tremendous ability to enjoy life
* Possibility of death of a child or miscarriage
* A liking for contact sports, either as participant or spectator
* The ability to make significant achievements in a particular area

## Sixth

* Vital need to work and serve
* Can be extremely hard worker and be a power threat to co-workers
* Interest in healing, often with a spiritual base
* Possible physical problems with blockages such as constipation
* Able to work in crisis occupations
* Best success would come through regenerative work

## Seventh

* Vital need for cooperation with a partner
* A desire for a sexually satisfying marriage
* Can attract powerful business partner
* Probable early marriage or elopement
* Possibility of marrying a powerful or strongly self-sufficient person

## Eighth

* Vital need to understand the meaning of life
* Powerful sex drive with strong sexual personality
* There can be concern over extremes of money
* Possible career in daring or dangerous field
* Often bestows logical, analytical business ability

## Ninth

* Vital interest in Ninth House matters of the higher mind-law, philosophy and religion
* Possible psychic ability

* Can overload the mind at times
* Highly developed intuition
* A love of exciting travel
* Great desire to use and expand abstract mind

Tenth

* Vital need for powerful career
* Desire to be "the boss"
* Career can involve life and death situations
* Strong drive for independence
* All this power needs discipline to use it in positive ways
* Power drive for success
* Very strong willpower

Eleventh

* Vital need for friends
* Friends can affect your career either positively or negatively
* There is often interest in occult subjects and groups
* Ability to influence friends
* Must strive to use this influence in a positive way
* Interest in reform

Twelfth

* Vital need to understand the meaning of life
* Strong intuition or psychic ability, which can be positively or negatively expressed
* If positively used, there can be great service to those in need
* If negatively used, there can be deep-rooted psychological problems, or difficulties with drugs and/or secret enemies
* Must guard against temptation.

# Aspects

Aspects are the engine parts of a birth Chart. They show you "where the action is." The type of Aspect tells you where the trouble lies, or where things will run smoothly. The more Aspects in a Chart, the more activity in life. Planets become stronger when contacts are made to them. An unaspected Planet makes me think of "The Farmer in the Dell" when "the cheese stands alone." The Planet without any Aspects will not be as strong as a Planet in Aspect to another Planet. The greater number of Aspects involving one Planet, the stronger and more prominent the Planet becomes.

There is one problem in trying to understand your Aspects without the aid of an astrologer, who integrates the Chart as a whole. This problem occurs when one Aspect is overpowered by two or more other Aspects to the same Planets. For example, the Moon in Opposition to Saturn indicates a sad, morose or melancholy personality, and a difficult life with many hardships. This Aspect appears in Chart II of the comparison of two women's Charts, who were born two days apart. The Moon in this Chart is Trine the Ascendant and Sextile Neptune in close orb, as well as the Opposition to Saturn. Saturn is Trine Neptune and Sextile the Ascendant. The personality in this case is cheerful and, aided by the Sagittarian Sun, is also optimistic. While hardships have existed in her life, there has been strength to overcome.

In trying to determine the strength of an Aspect, remember that the closer the orb, the stronger the influence. Also, if you have a computerized Chart, the Aspects are often listed with an A or S after them. "A" stands for applying, meaning that the Planets were approaching an exact orb at the moment of birth. "S" stands for separating, meaning that the Planets were separating from an exact orb, and therefore not quite as strong as an approaching Aspect.

The Aspects in this section are written in a graphic, outline form. This was designed as a quick reference tool. If you wish to read more detailed descriptions, you could use the books recommended earlier.

A large number of Aspects is an indication of a very busy life and/ or complex person. In some old astrology books, the hard Aspects are descibed in very negative terms. Astrologer Don Jacobs has an excellent way of distinguishing between the hard and ease Aspects. He says, "Any Aspect of Venus and Mars, for instance, is going to make you sexy. The strength of the angle and your ability to handle the sexiness depends on the angle. The difference is not in kind, it's only more or less of the same thing."

### Sun with the Moon:

| Conjunction* | Sextile, Trine | Square, Opposition |
|---|---|---|
| Focused interests | Easygoing, without much | Strong drive for success |
| Strong emphasis by | ambition | Opinionated |
| Sign and House | Self-confidence | Lack of perspective |
| Lack of adaptability | Vitality | Instability |
| Tendency toward | Harmonious personality | Inner conflicts |
| isolation | Attraction to opposite sex | Difficult marriage |
| Self-opinionated | Success is often without | Mental ability |
| Driving will | struggle | especially in Opposition |

## *Conjunction of the Sun and Moon

When the Sun and Moon are Conjunct, it is a crucial placement as these are the two most important Planets. The Sun, which represents our active, masculine side, usually overpowers the Moon, which indicates our receptive, feminine instincts. The Sign and House placements become very important, as the individual focuses his/her energies in that House and Sign. With this Conjunction, the Aspects from other Planets to the Sun or Moon are usually the same. Mercury, and often Venus, can be found in the same House or Sign (since neither Planet is ever very far from the Sun). So, there can almost be a tunnel vision effect in the direction or career of the person. This can be seen in the Bowl Chart of the woman attorney from Washington, D.C. where her focus is the Eighth House (investigation and digging to the bottom of things).

## Sun with Mercury:

Because of the closeness of the two Planets (never more than 28° apart), there can only be two possible Aspects, the Conjunction, and the very minor aspect call a Semi-Sextile. The Semi-Sextile occurs when two Planets are 30° from each other. Its meaning would be a watered-down version of a Sextile.

## Conjunction

Strong, healthy optimistic mind
Inclines toward material interests
Independent thinker
Can be conceited
Lacks adaptability
When the Conjunction is less than 3°,
the mind can occasionally "short
circuit" like an overloaded electrical wire
Subjective opinions

## The Semi-Sextile

Intelligent
Clear perceptions
Smooth mental flow
Ingenious
Healthy mind

### Sun with Venus:

(Never more than 48° apart, so the only Aspects possible are the Conjunction and the Semi-Sextile).

## Conjunction

People oriented
Attractive
Affectionate
Cheerful, warm hearted
Artistic
May lack drive for worldly success
Desire for popularity

## The Semi-Sextile

Ability to attract
Artistic and/or apprecia-
tion of the arts
Affectionate
Social
Good taste

## Sun with Mars:

### Conjunction

Energetic, can be
hyperactive
This gives an Aries
influence to the Sun
Sign, making the
person very asser-
tive
Strong ego identi-
fication
Very hard working
Possibility of prob-
lems from injury or
disease
Very competitive
Tremendous creative
talent
Problems caused by
always asserting
your own will
Desire for constant
action needs to be
balanced with rest

### Sextile, Trine

Energetic
Harmonious flow of
energy
Well balance ego
In a woman - it makes
her attractive to men

Leadership ability

Good physical
coordination
Alert, quick

Objective/Decisive
Enjoys physical and mental
activity/always busy
Courage/Enthusiasm
Self-control
Always able to use creative
abilities
Capable of handling difficult
or demanding jobs

### Square, Opposition

Stressful energy
Antagonistic
Opinionated
Likes to contradict
others

Combative/reckless
Restless/impatient

Lack of restraint
Tendency to overwork

Possible health problems
in Opposition
Strong drive for success
Powerful sexual nature
requires a compatible
mate

## Sun with Jupiter:

### Conjunction

One of the most beneficial
Aspects
Good health/Vigor
Brings ambition with 9th
House matters
Decisive/Expressive
Much more ambitious than
ease Aspects
Tremendous enthusiasm

### Sextile, Trine

Primarily an intellectual
power Aspect
Interest in philosophy
and law
Spiritual influence
Good health
This ease Aspect often
hinders full development
of abilities, as there
is little personal ambition

Generous
Traveling is usually of the
restful kind, with short
visits with friends

### Square, Opposition

Jupiter, even in
stressful Aspects, does
not act inharmoniously

These two Planets in
friction often denote
accomplishments and the
striving for success
Sluggish circulation
Dislike of routine
Tendency to ignore
convention
Health problems could
develop through
excesses in the diet

## Sun with Saturn:

### Conjunction

Inhibits and hides the Sun
qualities
Usually makes the person
very quiet
Can aid career achievement
if positive
Work often done in seclusion
Ability to handle great
responsibility
Self-control

### Sextile, Trine

Ambitious
Good bones and teeth
Long life
Benefits career
Works well under rules
and laws
Self-control
Very conservative
Success comes from hard
work
Painstaking analytical
ability
Able to handle
responsibility
Indicator of good health

### Square, Opposition

Lack of self confidence
A difficult Aspect in
careers, causing slow
development
Problems with bones or
teeth
Does not like
restrictions
Pessimistic
Overly cautious
Inhibits use of abilities
Success comes slowly
through sheer hard work
after starting at the bottom

## Sun with Uranus:

| Conjunction | Sextile, Trine | Square, Opposition |
|---|---|---|
| Extremely creative | Originality | Inhibits creativity |
| Unusual or different type | Constant flow of creative | Stressful energy |
| of person | ideas | Often extreme self-will |
| A need to release energy | Magnetic appeal | Problems in making |
| through working with | Sudden bursts of energy | correct judgments |
| metal (machines, computers, | A leadership Aspect | |
| typewriters, musical | | Life seems to be full of |
| instruments with metal parts | Independent | upsets |
| art forms involving metal) | Often connected with some | |
| | unusual movement or | Rebellious attitude |
| Benefits literary or scientific | cause | toward authority |
| career | Natural dramatic flair | Can be arrogant |
| | A powerful speaker | |
| High nervous energy | Good emotional strength | |
| | Well balanced ego | |

## Sun with Neptune:

| Conjunction | Sextile, Trine | Square, Opposition |
|---|---|---|
| Makes you "other worldly" | Attractive | Self deception |
| Imagination | Spiritual | Inhibits imagination |
| Often interested in music | Harmony with inner | Possible dependence on |
| Drawn toward mystical and | beliefs | drugs or alcohol |
| spiritual matters | Creative imagination | Often vulnerable |
| Lack of confidence | Ability to envision things | Possible misuse of |
| Creativity in the arts | Love of water and the sea | psychic ability |
| | Sensitive desire to help | Creative imagination, |
| | people in need | but problems expressing |
| | | it |

## Sun with Pluto:

| **Conjunction** | **Sextile, Trine** | **Square, Opposition** |
|---|---|---|
| Tremendous power | Powerful, balanced ego | Power struggles |
| Extremes in opinions | Great strength | Difficulties with people |
| and behavior | Ability to accomplish | in authority |
| Thirst for powerful | Courage | Great feelings of |
| position in life | Great vitality | frustration |
| Capable of great success | Natural leader | Tendency to have a chip |
| when you use your | Talent with 8th House | on your shoulder |
| abilities to help others | activities | Executive ability in |
| Strong sex drive | Tremendous creative | Square |
| | ability | Very defensive in |
| | Intuitive perception | Opposition |
| | | Must learn to compro- |
| | | mise |

## Sun with the Ascendant:

| **Conjunction** | **Sextile, Trine** | **Square, Opposition** |
|---|---|---|
| A need to be important | Self-confidence | Possible problems with |
| Self-confidence | Strong indication of | relationships |
| If Sun is in the 1st House, | public recognition | The Square indicates |
| there will be great vitality | Harmonious, magnetic | tension and stress |
| and too much focus on the | personality | Can come on too strongly |
| self | Pleasant relationships | The Opposition indicates |
| If Sun is in the 12th House, | with others | a strong interest in |
| there is a tendency to | Desire to be important | partnerships when the |
| withdraw from the spotlight, | Natural ease and command | Sun is in the 7th House |
| work behind the scenes | of expression | |
| The Ascending Sign qualities | Open and aboveboard | If the Sun is in the 6th |
| will be strongly pronounced | Creative ability | House, there can be |
| Personal striving for | Strength and vitality | health problems |
| recognition | Possible lack of drive | Difficulty in balancing |
| Physical strength | in career | the basic character |
| Good health, or quick | | with the personality |
| recuperation from occasional | | |

illness

# Sun with the Midheaven:

| Conjunction | Sextile, Trine | Square, Opposition |
|---|---|---|
| Ability to obtain prominence | Well adjusted public image | Struggle with attitude toward career |
| Desire for public recognition | | |
| Completely at ease with career choice, unless there are hard Aspects to this Conjunction | Ability to recognize your career potentials and limitations | Possible problems between career and family |
| A need to establish personal identity | Positive outlook on life | Unclear career goals |
| Strong focus on career | Opportunities to advance your career | A satisfactory family relationship must be achieved in order to have a productive career |
| Well balanced ego | Well-regulated career and home life | |
| Able to influence others | Family will be supportive toward your career | |
| Indicator of fame | Indicator of career success | Difficulties with authority figures |
| | | Problems with public reputation |

# ASPECTS OF THE MOON

# Moon with Mercury:

| Conjunction | Sextile, Trine | Square, Opposition |
|---|---|---|
| Often indicates high intelligence | Harmonious emotional expression | Sharp intellect, even more so than the Trine or Sextile |
| Mental judgment can be colored by emotions | Common sense | Independent thinker |
| Penetrating mind | Shrewd mind | Sensitive |
| Powerful imagination | Kind disposition | Strain between the emotions and mentality |
| Very active mind | Mind is usually logical and honest | |
| Sensitive and sympathetic | Good for all forms of communication | Actively sympathetic |
| People feel comfortable with you | Good memory | Strong loyalty |
| | Lively imagination | Restless, highstrung |
| | High level of comprehension | Can cause criticism or even slander against you |

## Moon with Venus

| Conjunction | Sextile, Trine | Square, Opposition |
|---|---|---|
| Refined manner | An innate ability to do | Problems with affections |
| Calm emotions | the right thing at | and/or partner's money |
| Love of the arts | the right time | Sometimes there is natu- |
| Good sense of perspective | Benefits artistic talent | ral disdain toward luxury |
| Possible extravagance | Sociability and popularity | |
| | Usually produces a charming | |
| | manner | |

## Moon with Mars:

| Conjunction | Sextile, Trine | Square, Opposition |
|---|---|---|
| Extremes in energy | Good flow of energy | Eruptions and strain be- |
| Strong Aries influence | between the two Planets | tween emotions and ac- |
| in the personality | | tions |
| | Courage | Rebellious |
| Daring types - risk | In women, as well as men, | Lack of physical strength |
| taker | it gives strength to | or prone to illness |
| Outgoing - likes direct | the body | Lack of self-control |
| contact | Kindhearted, nurturing | Tends toward independ- |
| Constructive action | Assertive and direct | ence |
| Enterprising | Usually adds depth to | Wants own career |
| | the mind | Impulsive |
| | | Resents opposition |

## Moon with Jupiter:

| Conjunction | Sextile, Trine | Square, Opposition |
|---|---|---|
| Powerful emotions | Rich emotional life | Emotional life under |
| | | stress |
| Strong nurturing instincts | Good nurturing instinct | Self-indulgent |
| More powerful than | Generous | Restless, easygoing |
| Trine or Sextile | Indicates goód health | Could be lazy |
| Practical ability | Successful, generous | Extremes in religious |
| | | beliefs |

| | | |
|---|---|---|
| Possible self-importance | Friendly and helpful | Lacks balance in business/money affairs |
| Very sympathetic | Usually bestows shrewd | |
| An indicator of good | business ability | Can also bring success |
| fortune as reward | Good-natured | Usually kind and generous |

## Moon with Saturn:*

| **Conjunction** | **Sextile, Trine** | **Square, Opposition** |
|---|---|---|
| Inhibits and hides emotions | Steady, strong emotions Sense of duty | Serious attitude Great depth in Opposition |
| Memories of the past are important | Patient Practical business sense | Cold responses to or from others |
| Very hard working | Conservative | Tendency to depression unless there are beneficial Aspects in Chart |
| Common sense Possible depression or melancholia | Expands imagination Men can be attracted to older women | Strain between home and career |
| Self-discipline | Strong organizing talent | Trouble letting go of unhappy memories Possible health problems Ambitious |

*       Any Aspect between the Moon and Saturn creates some difficulties - from solitary work (this does not necessarily mean loneliness) to hardships in life.

## Moon with Uranus:

| **Conjunction** | **Sextile, Trine** | **Square, Opposition** |
|---|---|---|
| Emotional tension Rapidly changing moods Unusual feelings Desire for excitement | Magnetic, vivacious personality Great determination Ambitious | Fierce independence Bestows ingenious talent High tension nerves Strong, sustained interest in some special or |

Need for independence
and the unconventional
Interests are always off
"the beaten path"

Great dislike of routine

Interest or talent in
astrology
Vivid imagination
A natural acceptance
of duties

Intuitive ideas

unusual subject

Restlessness
Often denotes high intel-
lect
Ability to follow your
own path

## Moon with Neptune:

| Conjunction | Sextile, Trine | Square, Opposition |
| --- | --- | --- |
| Spiritual inclination | Gifted imagination | Confusion of emotional |
| Psychic, intuitive | Sympathetic | feelings |
| Impressionable | Acting talent | Nervous strain |
| Tendency towards | Highly intuitive and | Emotional tension |
| seclusion | psychic | Possible lack of common |
| | | sense |
| Self-sacrificing | Possible photographic | Easily frustrated |
| Difficulty in keeping | memory | Self-deception and |
| emotions balanced | | possibility of deception |
| | Artistic abilities | to, or from,  others |
| Sympathetic and kind | Desire to do something | |
| | outstanding | Possibility of scandal |
| A tendency toward | | |
| secret affairs, or | A spiritual influence | |
| the extreme of | | |
| religious fervor | | |

## Moon with Pluto:

| Conjunction | Sextile, Trine | Square, Opposition |
| --- | --- | --- |
| Powerful feelings | Intense feelings | Expression of emotions |
| Impulsive | Prohibits draining of | often blocked |
| Desire to dominate | of emotional energy | Sudden outbursts |
| others emotionally | Good sense of humor | Fierce drive for emotional |
| Strong need for emotional | Constructive use of | power |
| fulfillment and control | emotional power | Can achieve power over |
| | | public thinking in a neg- |
| Capable of very deep love | Psychic ability | ative way |

Can be difficult to live
with

Strong sexual desires

Dislike of anything
superficial

Great depth of emotions

Enjoyment of children
Good money manager

Demanding attitude can
cause problems with
friends

Need to learn to compro-
mise

## Moon with the Ascendant:

| **Conjunction** | **Sextile, Trine** | **Square, Opposition** |
|---|---|---|
| The emotions strongly affect the personality reflecting the Ascendant's Sign | Harmonious expression of emotions | Emotional upsets or problems |
| | Well balanced emotions | Hinders self-expression |
| In the 1st House, the emotions are very prominent | Strong imagination | Uncomfortable or awkward style of communicating with people |
| | Benefits communication in social and domestic arenas | |
| In the 12th House, the emotions are hidden, and there is need for seclusion | | Career difficulties |
| | Strong creative ability | Very impressionable and emotionally vulnerable |
| | Resourceful intellect | Dislike of competition |
| Emotional strength | Pleasant, good-natured disposition | Tendency to become too involved in other people's affairs |
| Vivid imagination | Your generosity needs appreciation | |
| Feminine mannerisms | Capable of utilizing talents | |
| Strong attachment to family | | |

## Moon with the Midheaven:

| **Conjunction** | **Sextile, Trine** | **Square, Opposition** |
|---|---|---|
| Fluctuations in career | Emotional expression benefits your career | Emotional problems or upsets involving your career |
| Possible career in food or home products | Cooperation in professional matters | Blocks effective communication in career and |

Popularity with the public
Beneficial placement for
people in the public eye

Ability to benefit career
through women

An indicator of success
in dealing with the
public

Able to deal easily with
the public
Sensitivity to the public
Smooth relationships with
career superiors

Success indicator
Pleasant home life

at home
Possible emotional problems with family
There could be problems
with your public reputation
In Opposition, there is
great attachment to the
home

## ASPECTS OF MERCURY

### Mercury with Venus:*

\*      Since these two Planets are never more than 76° apart, the only Aspects are the Conjunction, the Sextile, the Semi-Sextile and the Semi-Square

| Conjunction | Sextile |
| --- | --- |
| Stronger than the Sextile in benefitting speech and writing | The manner of speaking and writing is charming |
| Healthy balance of nerves | Cheerful |
| Pleasant manner of expression | Social |
| Intellectual offspring | Artistic ability in craftsmanship |
| Social grace | Enjoyment of young people |
| Diplomatic | Talent in verbal or written communication |
| | Skill in using your talents |
| | Prefers light mental topics |

### Mercury with Mars:

| Conjunction | Sextile, Trine | Square, Opposition |
| --- | --- | --- |
| Great mental energy | Gives power to the mind | Sharp intellect |
| Talent for satire | Sharp sense of hearing and sight | Tendency to overwork |
| Mental courage | Common sense | Nervous mental energy, carried to extreme can cause nervous exhaustion |
| Benefits writing ability of Mars-related topics | Incisive mind | |
| Aggressive | Inclines toward literary offspring | Irritable |
| Willingness to debate | Quick ability to "size up" opponents | Combative |
| Sincerity | | Intelligence is often not fully used |
| Restless mind | | |
| Tendency to interrupt | | |

## Mercury with Jupiter:

### Conjunction

Above average intelligence

Interest in law, art, religion and abstract thought

Lacks ambition
Good-natured, but sometimes conceited
Common sense
Generous, kind thoughts of others
Optimistic

Enjoyment of original or investigative thinking done in seclusion

Dislike of detailed work

### Sextile, Trine

The mind is active and sharp, but not necessarily ambitious

Good-natured

Sense of humor
While not an Aspect for achievement, it seems to eliminate financial worries
Interests lie in intellecual matters, rather than material goods
Usually good at book learning

### Square, Opposition

Active and fertile mind, but tends toward absent-mindedness

Poor judgment caused by too broad an optimistic outlook
Aids artistic or writing talents
Possible losses through dishonesty of others
In stress situations, mental resources do not function well

Impulsive judgment
Tendency to shortcut learning


## Mercury with Saturn:

### Conjunction

Great powers of concentration
Good mental retention
Methodical, perceptive mind
Solitary habits

Possible depression
Slow development of intellect and career
If the rest of the Chart does not show energy, this can cause mental inertia

### Sextile, Trine

Aids practical mentality
Ambitious, hard working
Good reasoning ability
Depth of thought
Well disciplined and organized thinking

Serious, methodical mind
Precision with words

Organizational ability
Detail oriented

### Square, Opposition

Rigid, serious mind
Outspoken and abrupt
Narrow-minded
Lack of ability for "small talk"
Limits success and friendships
Possible depression
Mind works hard in making decisions

There is usually limitation in life

## Mercury with Uranus:

| **Conjunction** | **Sextile, Trine** | **Square, Opposition** |
|---|---|---|
| Mentally independent | Original thinker | Outspoken |
| Genius possible | Quick, keen mind | Lacking in tact |
| Alert, quick mind | Dramatic speaking ability | Good inventive mind, but not the ability to present |
| Fluid speech | Very good memory | ideas well |
| Interest in new ideas | Intuitive | |
| Progressive thinker | Can instill great ingenuity | Easily irritated |
| Colorful manner | and even genius | Nonconformist |
| of expression | Good influence for | The ability to excite and |
| Powerful will | popularity | stimulate others |

## Mercury with Neptune:

| **Conjunction** | **Sextile, Trine** | **Square, Opposition** |
|---|---|---|
| Clairvoyant | Creative imagination | Active imagination |
| Vivid imagination | Kind, gentle disposition | Absent-minded |
| Very impressionable | Dislike of rough behavior | Sensitive perceptions |
| Sensitive intellect | Good sense of humor | Attracted to the arts |
| Subtle, romantic, or | Writing ability | Confusion in thinking |
| poetic types | Intuitive, artistic mind | Can be deceptive |
| Talent in music, writing, | Possible interest in | Strong need to express |
| or photography | spiritual and/or occult | ideas and feelings |
| Must guard against illusion | matters | Speech can be very cir- |
| and delusion | | cuitous |
| | Memory often photo- | Indecisive |
| | graphic | |
| Possible ability in water | Strong powers of | Can be naive |
| sports or activities | visualization | |

## Mercury with Pluto:

**Conjunction**

Intense mind
Always sees reality
Strong probing,
investigating mind
Can be cynical
Potential for powerful
mental development
Possible power drive
Speaking ability

Dislike of weakness
Psychic ability

**Sextile, Trine**

Analytical
Resourceful intellect
Vast intellect
Powerful speaking ability
Competitive
Penetrating mind
Strong mental energy
Brings success
Able to influence
others

Good mediator
Talent in 8th House matters

**Square, Opposition**

Penetrating thoughts
Brutally frank
Problem-solving ability
Lack of mental balance
Mentally daring
Good Aspect for investi-
gating and/or research
Secretive and suspicious
Need to learn concentra-
tion and mental disci-
pline

## Mercury with the Ascendant:

**Conjunction**

Tremendous mental
activity
Pleasure in communication
Ability in speaking
or writing
Often bestows outstanding
intelligence, which can
produce prominence

Very preoccupied with
yourself

**Sextile, Trine**

Desire to exchange thoughts
with others
Precise, clear speech
Speaking and writing skills
Sharp senses in Sextile
Instinctive, analytical
ability

Love of learning and
communicating

**Square, Opposition**

Tendency to make
comments about others -
gossip
Difficulty in expressing
ideas

Lack of confidence which
can be hidden by arro-
gance
Possible delays in educa-
tion which can be over-
come

Must learn positive thinking

## Mercury with the Midheaven:

| Conjunction | Sextile, Trine | Square, Opposition |
| --- | --- | --- |
| Career involvement with communications | Ability in developing skills for career | Possible problems in education which could affect career |
| Enjoyment of business conversation | Smooth communication skills which can benefit home and career | Hindrance toward success in career |
| Writing talent | | |
| Original thinking | | Difficulties in communication with family members and career associates |
| Indicator of public speaking ability | Harmony between career and family life | |
| Mind focuses on career | Writing talent connected to career | Problems in writing which involve career |

# ASPECTS OF VENUS

## Venus with Mars:*

| Conjunction | Sextile, Trine | Square, Opposition |
|---|---|---|
| Social charm | Graceful balance of | Powerful passions |
| Intensifies emotion | sexuality | Can be hypersensitive |
| Passionate sexual drive | Affectionate, warm- | Strongly attracted to |
| Strong attraction to, and | hearted | opposite sex when in |
| from the opposite sex | Talent in working with | Square; problems relat- |
| | the hands in fields | ing to the opposite sex |
| Vigorous love of life | related to beauty and | in Opposition |
| Sensuous | adornment | |
| Sense of fun | | Impulsive and/or irritable |
| | Energetic | Warmly affectionate |
| | Sex appeal | Disappointed by other |
| | | people's lack of kind- |
| | Ability to relate well | ness |
| | with the opposite sex | |
| | and children | |

* The contact of these two Planets brings enjoyment of children, music and dancing.

## Venus with Jupiter:

| Conjunction | Sextile, Trine | Square, Opposition |
|---|---|---|
| Very affectionate | Similar to the Conjunction, | Vanity |
| Generous | but with more outward | Self-indulgence |
| Charming | reach | Desire to be the center of |
| Popular | Spiritual awareness | attention |
| Lucky and fortunate | Ability in artistic careers | Craving for luxury |
| Interest in religion, | A genuine liking of people | Extravagant, flowery |
| speech and philanthropy | Charming manner of | speech |
| Teaching ability | expression and voice | |
| | | Problems can come from |
| Intense love of beauty | Natural grace | over-expansion |
| Polished speaking ability | Popularity | Tendency to be a front- |
| | | runner |

## Venus with Saturn

| **Conjunction** | **Sextile, Trine** | **Square, Opposition** |
|---|---|---|
| Inhibits sociability | Outstanding artistic | Disappointments in love |
| Long-lasting relationships | talents | Problems expressing emotions |
| Inability to express love | Serious expression of love | Lonely, melancholy disposition |
| Strong sense of duty and loyalty | | Selfish |
| Miserly | Long-lasting marriage | Lack of social graces |
| Possible career in artistic fields | Social activities are usually business-related | Often shy and inhibited Problems in relating to others |
| Money can be slow in coming | Strong sense of responsibility | More interest in practical matters rather than social ones |
| Disappointments in love and romance | Thrifty with money which builds slowly | Marriage could be to an older person for money rather than love |
| | Business ability | |
| | Duties are willingly performed, often with spiritual understanding | |
| | Will sacrifice for loved ones | |

## Venus with Uranus:

| **Conjunction** | **Sextile, Trine** | **Square, Opposition** |
|---|---|---|
| Sparkling, magnetic personality | Exciting, outgoing personality | Love relations can be exciting, but unstable |
| Sudden, unconventional attractions | Popularity | Possibility of brief marriages |
| | Lucky in love | Magnetic and charming, but selfish |
| Possible original, artistic talent | Attractive to the opposite sex | |
| | | Often fickle |
| Risk takers, with erratic behavior | Gifted in artistic areas and/or great love of the arts | Fierce desire for personal freedom |
| Love relations are often more group-connected | | Unusual love attractions and urges |
| Quick coming and going | Optimistic, happy attitude attracts friends | Extreme tension in emo- |

of money

Can be self-willed
pleasure seeker
Intense emotional nature

Desire for exciting romance
Can be eccentric in love
relationships

tional life

Nervous irritability

## Venus with Neptune:

### Conjunction

Spiritual, ethereal
quality
Frequent psychic ability
Wonderful power of
attraction
Very sensitive

Ability in music, art,
photography
Impractical, naive
Romantic and idealistic
in love relationships
The romantic dreamer

### Sextile, Trine

Elegant expression of love
Artistic imagination
Good taste
Possibility of finding
soul mate
Love of the arts and music

Attraction to relaxed
career in the arts or
helping others
Problem-solving ability
Kind and compassionate
Dislike of routine hard
work

### Square, Opposition

Possible unwise love
Unrealistic attitudes
Disillusion in love
Self-deception
Indecision
Can be led astray or de-
ceived
There is a possibility of
scandal from unusual love
relationships
Can be lazy
Aesthetic appreciation

## Venus with Pluto:

### Conjunction

Magnetic personality

Fanatic love feelings

Great need to control
passions
Deep, intense emotions
Very demanding attitude
toward, and from,
partner
Possible blockage of

### Sextile, Trine

Powerful capacity for love

The "peacemaker"

Intense ability to create
Tremendous power of
attraction
Outstanding artistic talent
with intense sensitivity
to color
Strong sexuality, but

### Square, Opposition

Excessive sexual expres-
sion
Problems in love relationships
Unless there is strength
of character in the Chart,
this could indicate pos-
sible sexual perversion
Financial problems if
risks are taken
Powerful sexual urges

affections

Tremendous sex appeal
Domination of social
circle
Intense sexuality

expressed in refined
way

Capacity to help family
and friends
A love relationship with
a strong fated connection

Possibility of a transform-
ing love experience
which can benefit your
understanding

## Venus with the Ascendant:

| Conjunction | Sextile, Trine | Square, Opposition |
|---|---|---|
| Good looks | Pleasant manner | Problems in expressing |
| Great charm | Love of beauty | feelings |
| Very sociable, but | Socially adept | A lack of good taste |
| calculating | Finds pleasure in love | Possible disharmonious |
| Popular | Too easygoing | personality in Square |
| Affectionate | Tendency to compromise | Insecure |
| Good taste | too easily | Poorly defined goals |
| Desire for luxury | Can be taken advantage of | Tendency to social climb |
| Clever at putting your | Desire for harmony in | Very sensitive |
| best foot forward | relationships | Venus in 7th House |
| Self-seeking | Diplomatic | indicates a successful |
|  |  | marriage |
| Pleasing manners | Cheerful personality |  |
| Ability to create | Indicates happy marriage | The Square indicates |
| attractive environment | or partnership | problems in relating to |
|  |  | others |

## Venus with the Midheaven:

| Conjunction | Sextile, Trine | Square, Opposition |
|---|---|---|
| Artistic career especially | A kind, pleasant image | Vanity |
| involving adornment - | Ability in the arts | Possible problems in |
| or career may involve | Discriminating appreciation | expressing feelings |
| public relations or | of art | An unsympathetic pub- |
| diplomacy |  | lic image |

A loving and/or attractive public image
Career often involves partnership

Socially ambitious
Able to attract money

A loving disposition
A happy love life
Warm feelings toward the public

Diplomatic skills
Social graces benefit career
Desire for an attractive home

Sense of style out of sync with the public
With Venus in the 4th House,
there is a desire for a beautiful home
Possible difficult relationship

## ASPECTS OF MARS

### Mars with Jupiter:

| **Conjunction** | **Sextile, Trine** | **Square, Opposition** |
|---|---|---|
| Very energetic | Law-abiding | Too impulsive |
| Optimistic | Ability in sports | High energy level, but |
| Ambitious "go-getter" | Physical strength | difficulty in finding |
| Love of life | Willpower | outlets for it |
| Quick coming and going | Desire for active life | Reckless, excitable |
| of money | Enthusiastic enjoyment | Tendency to short-cut the |
| | of life | law |
| Power of concentration | | Too fearless |
| toward objective | Religious and humanitarian | Hard worker in need of |
| Frequently involved in | interests | discipline |
| disputes | Ability to work with | Possible muscular prob- |
| | young people | lems |
| Impulsive actions | | Lack of moderation |
| Quick tempered | Hard working | This is a difficult Aspect, |
| Ego - need to feel you | Optimistic | especially in Opposition, |
| know everything | Loyal | which needs work to |
| Outspoken | The material aspects of | control |
| Can be belligerent | life are usually | |
| | comfortable | |

### Mars with Saturn:

| **Conjunction** | **Sextile, Trine** | **Square, Opposition** |
|---|---|---|
| Accident-prone | Great endurance | Too self-willed |
| Saturn constricts the | Organizing ability | Saturn restricts Mars |
| Mars urge for action | | courage, producing |
| | Physical strength and | fearfulness |
| Usually needs lots of sleep | and disipline | Energy is blocked which |
| | | can cause violent erup- |
| Hard worker | Ability to overcome | tions |
| Physical stamina | hardships (as in | Impatient |
| Possible suppression of | pioneering) | Career problems because |
| anger | Courageous | of unfocused sex drive |
| Energy focused on career | Success comes through | Limits sex drive |
| Saturn restricts Mars | discipline, hard work | Intolerant |

aggressive tendencies

Tremendous willpower
Efficient use of energy

Energy is like a traffic
light - starts and stops

## Mars with Uranus:

**Conjunction**

**Sextile, Trine**

**Square, Opposition**

Great energy, but with
tremendous tension
Craves excitement
The Aspect of the
daredevil and
thrill seeker
Fearless, daring,
courageous
The "revolutionary"
Very alert and quick
This energy needs
direction
Works best in dangerous
situations
Muscular strength
Strong willpower

Lack of patience

Quick, good action
Courageous without
being foolish
Sudden, great energy
Inventive, original
Hard, fast worker
Ability to achieve one
goal after another
Great enthusiasm
Strong, magnetic sexual
drive
Physical strength
Dramatic expression
Career must allow great
freedom
Ability to deal with
difficult situations

Accident prone
Dislike of routine
Nervous tension
Impatient, impulsive
Possible danger in risk-
taking situations
Tendency to argue and
contradict
Interest in thrill sports
Leadership ability
Can be ruthless
Strong sexual impulses
Intense drive to have your
own way
Can overwork
Unusual in some way:
either off-beat or eccen-
tric, or unconventional

## Mars with Neptune:

**Conjunction**

**Sextile, Trine**

**Square, Opposition**

Powerful imagination
Weakens the physical
energy of muscles
Artistic ability,
especially with colors

Enthusiasm may lack
control or follow-
through
Can be involved in deceit
or fraud
Dislike of hard work

Able to act effectively
on intuition
Powerful emotions
Honest, but secretive
Ability to attract people
to your beliefs

Interest in meditative
exercises
Good Aspect for water-
related careers
Psychic ability

Weakened physical drive
Actions through hidden
motivation
Religious leadership
Possible problems with
drugs or alcohol

Tendency to misuse
physical energy
Creative imagination
Susceptible to deceit
Lack of effective
planning

Magnetically attractive

Needs a creative outlet
for this energy
Actions can be secretive

Love of romantic things

Good control of emotions

Sexual attractiveness
Desire to give practical
help

The ability to spot a
"phony"

Often ability in the arts,
as actor, dancer, singer
or artist

Usually slow to admit
mistakes
Possible irrational fears
Capable of bullying

## Mars with Pluto:

| Conjunction | Sextile, Trine | Square, Opposition |
|---|---|---|
| Incredible energy | Tremendous self-confidence | People with this Aspect can come on like "gang busters" |
| Great courage | Physical strength used | |
| Desire to use force | constructively | Too impulsive |
| Combative | Courageous leadership | Hot-tempered |
| Strong self-confidence | ability | Obsessive tendencies |
| Volatile temper which | Very ambitious | Powerful sex drive |
| must be controlled | Dynamic | Capable of using physical force |
| Tremendous endurance | Often involved in muscular | |
| Intense sexual energy | exercises | Great strength to overcome |
| Highly emotional | A natural inclination | |
| Magnetic appeal | for hard work | Ruthless pursuit of goals |
| Ability to use all your | Harmonious flow of | Frustration can cause |
| strengths in times of | physical and sexual | unpleasant behavior |
| crisis | energy | |

## Mars with the Ascendant:

| Conjunction | Sextile, Trine | Square, Opposition |
|---|---|---|
| Live-wire energy | Energetic | Can be too aggressive |
| Impulsive | Forceful | Quick-tempered |
| Impetuous | Nervous energy | Unwilling to submit to |
| Energy directed to areas | Hard worker | others' authority |
| related to Ascendant | Competitive | Capacity to work hard |
| Sign | | toward goals |
| | Tremendous enthusiasm | Tendency to be competitive with everyone |

| | | |
|---|---|---|
| Aggressive | Talkative | Control of "fighting in- stinct" is necessary to fully develop talents |
| Quick-tempered | Need for long-range | |
| Zest for life | planning and discipline | |
| Appearance of confidence | Can be a successful leader | Frequent involvement in |
| Competitive | Benefits marriage and | disputes |
| Usually produces a need | partnerships | |
| to be a leader | Strengthens body | Problems in relationships |
| Muscular strength | Impulsive | |

## Mars with the Midheaven:

| **Conjunction** | **Sextile, Trine** | **Square, Opposition** |
|---|---|---|
| Tremendous energy in career | Well-directed energy in career | Problems in career and home life |
| Ability for successful career | Lively | Possible nervous tension in career |
| | Career success indicator | |
| Talent in Mars-related areas of weapons and knives (an Aspect of the surgeon) | Decision making ability | Upsets and arguments with job superiors or family members |
| | A talent for organization | |
| | The ability to use your | Business disappoint- |
| Great concentration on career | energy constructively | ments |
| | | Excitable |
| | Career may be operated | Emotional stress |
| | out of your home | A feeling of strain through |
| Independent | Desire for prominence | work |
| Capacity for hard work toward career goals | in career field | Difficulties with legal authorities |
| Very competitive | Hard working | |
| Need to obtain prominence | | |

# ASPECTS OF JUPITER

## Jupiter with Saturn:

| Conjunction | Sextile, Trine | Square, Opposition |
|---|---|---|
| This powerful Aspect occurs every 18 to 21 years | Self-confident | This Aspect slows success |
| Good business ability | Capacity for long-range planning | A lack of focused direction in career |
| Strong Aspect indicating ability to achieve success | Industrious | A possible poor self-image |
| Realistic goals | A career success indicator | Inhibits expression |
| Great capacity for hard work | Steady progress in life | Problems recognizing limitations |
| When Jupiter appears ahead of Saturn (in a lesser degree of longitude), Saturn tends to impose hardships, making success slower in coming | Ability to recognize limits of expansion and restriction | Success eventually comes through hard work |
| | Integrity | Restless |
| | Possible career in religion, law, or publishing | Narrows religious and philosophical outlook |
| | Very responsible | Usually gives the ability to accept disipline |
| | Indicates high standing as a person of honesty and wisdom | A lack of enthusiasm |
| When Saturn appears ahead of Jupiter, success comes more easily, but still through hard work | Discriminate generosity | Almost constant setbacks in response to initiative, which can cause depression |
| Physical endurance | Constructive power | |
| Easily irritated | An Aspect of material success | |

## Jupiter with Uranus:

| Conjunction | Sextile, Trine | Square, Opposition |
|---|---|---|
| This Aspect occurs every 14 years | Magnetic | Willful and restless |
| Unconventional | Strong leadership ability in humanitarian areas | Desire for unrealistic goals |
| Independent | Often brings incredible | Can be too outspoken |
| | | Interferes with logical |

Original, creative energy
Great interest in new and
progressive thinking
A flair for sensing trends
which benefits a career
in promotion or advert-
ising

Very enthusiastic
Resourceful
Possible unusual religious
beliefs

good luck in areas of
the Houses involved
Great originality
A great liking for the
unconventional

There is usually an
interest in contemporary
philosophies and religion

Possible sudden success
Intense love of, and respect
for, personal liberty

thinking
A lack of discipline
Obstinate in beliefs
Tendency to exaggerate
Must guard against specu-
lation
Religious beliefs are usu-
ally contrary to popular
religious opinions

## Jupiter with Neptune:

### Conjunction

This Conjunction occurs
every 13 years
Mystical tendencies

Very sympathetic
Talent and/or interest in
the arts
Great sensitivity in the
area of life by House
placement

Unusual psychic ability
Gifted imagination
Strong idealism
Abstract thinking often
has emotional base
Great potential that
needs developing

### Sextile, Trine

Rich intense imagination
Pronounced love of man-
kind
Strong religious tendencies
Artistic ability
Energy for good works
Enjoyment of meditation
A need for periods of
retreat and contemplation

Possible lack of common
sense
Extreme compassion
Indicator of psychic ability
Hospitable

### Square, Opposition

Easily led astray
Extreme sensitivity to
the suffering of others

Problems with practical
thinking
Creative ability
Confusion from emotions
Tendency towards wander-
lust
Lack of self-discipline
Problems with emotional
control
Desire for speculation
can cause money problems

## Jupiter with Pluto:

| Conjunction | Sextile, Trine | Square, Opposition |
|---|---|---|
| This Conjunction occurs every 12-13 years Great leadership This is an extremely powerful Aspect expressed through the Houses and Sign involved | Great talent in organization Exuberant, enthusiastic love of life Spiritual leadership ability and desire Intellectual wisdom Adaptability to new ways | A desire to force spiritual beliefs on others Fanatical approach to goals Tendency to wastefulness Fierce desire for power A lack of respect for the law Possible loss of fortunes |
| Tremendous drive for achievement Intense love of life Strengthens willpower Spiritual regeneration which can benefit you and others | Good health Powerful abilities for your career Tremendous strength to bring about spiritual regeneration to mankind Penetrating mental ability | Sexual excesses unless restraint is shown elsewhere in the Chart If this power is used selfishly, life can be lonely and unhappy Problems in judgment connected with money |
| Intense powers of concentration with the abstract mind Outstanding ability in problem solving at times of crisis Prophetic and psychic tendencies | Innate sense of right and wrong Ethical standards | Guard against any illegal involvements |

## Jupiter with the Ascendant:

| Conjunction | Sextile, Trine | Square, Opposition |
|---|---|---|
| An enthusiastic, outgoing personality Cheerful Optimistic Career interests may include religion, law, or philosophy | A very harmonious personality An Aspect of popularity Good fortune in dealing with the public | Problems in dealing with the public An awkward method of self expression Overly optimistic of how much you can handle A possible inflated opin- |
| When Jupiter is in the 12th House, there is often an | Enthusiastic attitude toward life | ion of yourself caused by an intense desire to be im- |
| | A lively personality | portant |

involvement in religion and/or behind-the-scenes service
When Jupiter is in the House, the personality is very jovial and expansive with a possiblity of taking on more than you can handle

Possible problems with excess weight
A desire for an attractive enviroment

Enjoyment of other people
Many career talents which need discipline to fully develop
Your contagious enthusiasm makes you a natural promoter

Indicator of a successful marriage or partnership

Generous

Pleasant manner of expression
An inclination to associate with important people

Possible difficutlies with marriage or business partners in Square Aspect
Good luck in marriage or partnership if Jupiter is in the 7th House in Opposition
A tendency to use people

Self-indulgent

## Jupiter with the Midheaven:

| **Conjunction** | **Sextile, Trine** | **Square, Opposition** |
|---|---|---|
| A great success indicator | A good Aspect for career success | An Aspect of self importance |
| An expansive, optimistic attitude toward your career | In Sextile, there will be many good opportunities | A tendency to spend too lavishly on your home Problems in viewing career objectively |
| Contentment with your public image A business reputation for honesty and integrity An Aspect of prominence in life A possible career in religion, law, politics, or higher education | to advance career Happiness in career and home life A reputation for honesty Possible career benefits through family Positive attitude toward career goals helps bring success | Difficulties in reaching career goals A strong desire and willingness to work for success Possible marriage or partnership problems unless Jupiter is in the 7th House Delusions of grandeur |
| Achievement in career The career is frequently in the public eye | A positive, cheerful attitude toward work and home life | |

## ASPECTS OF SATURN

### Saturn with Uranus:*

\* Because Uranus moves so slowly, this Aspect occurs in the Charts of people born within the same approxiamte two year span.

| Conjunction | Sextile, Trine | Square, Opposition |
|---|---|---|
| This Conjunction occurs about every 91 to 92 years | Strong willpower | Feelings of severe tension and strain |
| The Saturn need for restriction and the Uranus urge for freedom causes nervous tension and stress | The ability to overcome continued obstacles Administrative ability Good concentration | A see-saw of discipline vs. fierce desire for freedom Rash actions cause problems or restraint hinders career |
| In a positive way, the Planets combined keep each other from acting at the extreme end of their normal expression Reliability and determination in career Strength and obstinacy An ability to use new and innovative methods within traditional businesses | Prolongs life Able to develop new and inventive ideas within the framework of traditional methods Possible scientific career Systematic Ability to use your good common sense Able to work with great patience | Stubborn A need to be always right Irritable There is often a lack of humility |

### Saturn with Neptune:

| Conjunction | Sextile, Trine | Square, Opposition |
|---|---|---|
| This Aspect occurs about every 35 to 36 years Constructive uses of the imagination Possible conflict between Saturn's materialism and Neptune's idealism | Strong, practical imagination Ambitious Ability to see through illusion and deceit Spiritual strength Imaginative ideas to help | Impractical tendencies Possible difficulties in dealing with reality Emotional strain Sense of security Inhibited and fearful Work is often done in |

An Aspect of the artist
or musician
Possible periods of
depression
The career could be done
in isolation, or away from
the public eye

A lack of reason when the
emotions are aroused

those in need help
themselves
Organizational talent
Career is often behind-
the-scenes
Good powers of concent-
tration
Idealistic

isolation
Distrust of others
Talent in the arts and
business can be developed
Disappointments may
incline you to drugs or alcohol

## Saturn with Pluto:*

* Since Pluto is so slow moving, this can be a generational influence

| **Conjunction** | **Sextile, Trine** | **Square, Opposition** |
|---|---|---|
| This Conjunction occurs about every 92 years Powerful self-control Very ambitious The ambition of Saturn flows harmoniously with the power of Pluto | A strong Aspect for a successful career Strengthens ambitions Deep powers of concentration Great determination Ability to perform difficult work | Difficulties and delays in career A possible lack of feeling toward others Problems can have a karmic connection |
| The strength of self-denial | Strong willpower used constructively | Career achievements occur only after hard and steady application to work |
| Possibility of great achievements through career | Leadership ability | Behavior is sometimes harsh |
| Work is often kept secret until it is accomplished | While the focus is strongly on the career, there is still a strong connection to the spiritual side of life | The power of Pluto can be used in a cold-hearted or brutal way Often must carry heavy burdens Poor value judgments |
| Magicians frequently have this Aspect | Capacity for intense, hard work | Power struggles |
| When the Planets are also involved in several hard Aspects, this power can be used negatively | Acceptance of responsibility | |

## Saturn with the Ascendant:

| Conjunction | Sextile, Trine | Square, Opposition |
|---|---|---|
| Saturn restricts the outward expression of the personality | Practical ability Personality functions well with career | Inhibits personality Possible periods of depression Self-conscious |
| Serious attitude toward relationships Responsible Conservative A lack of self-confidence | Efficient Precise speech An indication of integrity Goal-oriented Deep understanding of others aids management skills | Feelings of frustration Pessimistic attitude toward life Defensive Difficulty in developing goals Remoteness caused by fear of being unaccepted |
| Possible problems with teeth and skin In the 1st House, there is a need for solitude An indicator of self-absorption Conversation tends toward serious matters only | Self discipline Strong sense of justice Very responsible Organizational talent Dignified manner | Limits friends The Square often causes marriage problems |

## Saturn with the Midheaven:

| Conjunction | Sextile, Trine | Square, Opposition |
|---|---|---|
| Powerful Aspect aiding the career, especially if placed in the 10th House Tremendous drive for success Focus can be centered so strongly on the career, that life can be lonely at the top An austere public image Capable of handling great responsibility Success achieved through long, hard work | A success indicator Practical ambition A slow, but steady climb to the top Strength to persevere Opportunities in life that aid career success The ability to learn from experience Benefits home and family life Strong organizational skills | Difficulties and obstacles in career Inhibition tends to limit ambition Feelings of frustration with career A lack of clear goals A plodding attitude in business Reliable in business Other responsibilities that impede success Family burdens Possible problems with employees |

# ASPECTS OF URANUS

## Uranus with Neptune:*

* Aspects between the three farthest out Planets (Uranus, Neptune and Pluto) are more important by House placement than Aspect. However, the Aspects between these Planets and the Ascendant or Midheaven are significant.

| Conjunction | Sextile, Trine | Square, Opposition |
|---|---|---|
| This Aspect occurs every 171 years This Conjunction last occurred in 1820; it will next occur in 1991-1993 This combination produces people with the great originality of Uranus combined with the kindness and sympathy of Neptune Gifted imagination Interest in spiritual and psychic matters The Aspect of the artistic genius | Idealistic Intuitive Sympathetic Original, artistic talent Sense of inner awareness Revolutionary ideas Interest in spiritual and mystical subjects Possible psychic ability Emotional enthusiasm for a cause Love of music and art Possible interest in the occult | Intense emotional level Impractical ideas Lack of control Excitable Instability Confused thinking High-strung Possible problems with involvement in occult matters Great need for a constructive outlet, possibly in the arts |

In Nature, the Square is connected to major disasters such as floods, earthquakes, storms and tornadoes. This Aspect was in effect in 1954 and 1955. The Opposition of these two Planets is even more powerful than the Square, causing major storms. These have ranged from severe hurricanes to devastating tidal waves. The last Opposition occurred from 1906 into 1911. The great San Francisco earthquake occurred in 1906.

## Uranus with Pluto:

### Conjunction

This Conjunction occurs about every 115 years
The last Conjunction was from 1963 to 1969
A powerful generational influence that produces innovative, revolutionary reform
Tremendous power for creating change
Strong respect for life
Spiritual energy
Interest in death and and life after death

### Sextile, Trine

Physical strength and endurance
Very inventive
The ability to use tremendous power and energy in a constructive way
Interest in spiritual
The placement of the Planets in the Houses will indicate areas of beneficial growth, especially if angular Houses are involved

### Square, Opposition

This Aspect indicates a period of time when drastic changes occurred in history
Eccentric
Explosive anger
Force without concern for consequences
Destructive tendencies
Tremendous tension
Can produce radical activists
Possible problems with misuse of occult matters

## Uranus with the Ascendant:

### Conjunction

The true eccentric
Usually bestows high intelligence
Nervous tension
Great personal magnetism
Strong intuitive ability
Originality in the Uranian areas of science or astrology
Revolutionary leadership ability
Very active and alert

### Sextile, Trine

Original, creative ability
Personal magnetism
The leaders in new trends
If Uranus is in the 5th House, there is great creative ability, and also tremendous sudden attractions in romance
Many opportunities for marriage
Lively, uninhibited personality

### Square, Opposition

If the Opposition is placed in the 7th House, it often indicates several marriages and divorces
Tremendous need for freedom
Interest in science, astrology, or the occult
A rebellious attitude
Sudden, exciting events in life
The Square causes problems in relationships

Possible scattering of
energy
Quick actions and reactions
Tremendous intuitive
ability

This Aspect makes you
stand out in a crowd
Outspoken in an
interesting way
Intuitive personality

Nonconformist attitude
Disregard for rules
Career must allow freedom
Desire for worthwhile work

## Uranus with the Midheaven:

| Conjunction | Sextile, Trine | Square, Opposition |
|---|---|---|
| Great originality in career | A career that allows a great deal of independence | Problems with career and home life |
| Unusual career energy | Outstanding talent in career | A tendency to act too impulsively |
| The Aspect of the inventor | Possibility of fame through originality | Nervous tension in career |
| The public image of the humanitarian | Friends frequently benefit the career | There can be sudden upsets in career |
| There can be sudden changes in career | Fame may come suddenly | Possible inability to conform |
| Interest in Uranian subjects of science, electronics or astrology | Strong organizing ability | There can be frequent changes of career and/or residence |
| The person who "does his own thing" | Great energy in striving toward career goals | Emotional upsets |
| Ability to use advanced ideas and procedures | A career success indicator | Rebellious attitude toward authority figures |
|  | Your home often reflects your originality |  |

# ASPECTS OF NEPTUNE

### Neptune with Pluto:

The Aspects of these two very slow-moving Planets are in orb for long periods of time. Their influence is very subtle. They are most significant in Aspect to the Ascendant or Midheaven

| Conjunction | Sextile, Trine | Square, Opposition |
|---|---|---|
| The last Conjunction occurred in the 1880's 1890's. It will occur again in the 24th century. A slow changing of deep-rooted attitudes It can awaken feelings of concern for humanity. It can be a time of great spiritual growth unless the Conjunction has several hard Aspects to it This Conjunction can mark major turning points in history | These Planets have been in Sextile Aspect since 1940 through all of this century. An interest in para-psychology Active imagination Opportunities for spiritual growth A constructive use of psychic or mystical gifts Idealistic attitude toward society Distaste for materialism | The last Square Aspect occurred in the early 1800's. It will occur again in the 21st century. The last Opposition was in 17th century. The next Opposition will occur in the 21st century. Wrong use of psychic abilities and occult matters A period of corruption A blockage in imaginative thinking A time of upheaval and moral decay |

### Neptune with the Ascendant:

| Conjunction | Sextile, Trine | Square, Opposition |
|---|---|---|
| Psychic ability The personality has a spiritual, mystical quality An ethereal and/or glamorous appearance Very imaginative | Artistic talent An attractive, graceful magnetic appearance An intriguing, charming personality Very sympathetic This can be an indicator | In Opposition, there can be danger from medical drugs if Neptune is in the 6th House If Neptune is in the 7th House, there can be an extreme idealistic attitude |

Great sensitivity to drugs and alcohol when Neptune is in the 1st House
When Neptune is in the 12th House, there can be escapism through drugs
A magnetic personality
Vulnerable
Artistic talent

of clairvoyance
An Aspect of popularity
Intuitive, sensitivity to others
Indicative of a happy marriage
Spiritual inclinations
Benefits marriage
Subtle personality

toward marriage
The Square is often an indicator of a deceptive personality
A lack of stamina
Illusions can cause disappointments
If Neptune is in the 7th House, be cautious of business partnerships

## Neptune with the Midheaven:

### Conjunction

An intriguing public image
A lack of career drive
Career often involved with the arts or spiritual matters
A dislike of routine work
Feelings of loneliness
The private or hidden part of the person is often revealed to the public
Acting or musical talent
Benefits career involving film or psychology

### Sextile, Trine

Imagination works well in career
Great interest in the arts
Intuitive ability aids career
Usually indicates a happy home life
Able to subtly influence authority figures
Career benefits for actors, musicians and artists
Effective subtle leadership ability
Naive

### Square, Opposition

Confused attitude toward career
Lack of confidence
Vulnerable to deception
Vague objectives in life
Possible problems with home life
A possible tendency toward laziness
Extreme sensitivity
Tendency to be unreliable in business
Disorganization in the home and career

# ASPECTS OF PLUTO

## Pluto with the Ascendant:

| Conjunction | Sextile, Trine | Square, Opposition |
| --- | --- | --- |
| Adds power and intensity to the personality Strengthens the characteristics of the Ascending Sign The desire for authority or power Physical stamina Strong intuitive ability All this power can be used for good or evil depending on the Chart as a whole Usually bestows good looks especially in men If Pluto is in the 12th House, there can be, deep-rooted psychological problems | The personality has a subtle charisma The Sextile brings opportunities to increase power The Trine brings ease in relating with others Strong ambition Good powers of concentration Possible clairvoyance Leadership ability Tremendous willpower Organizational ability Can wield power over masses of people in constructive ways Great self confidence Capable of initiating successful projects | Thirst for power The tendency to dominate the partner by force Very aggressive personality If Pluto is in the 6th House, there can be an obscure psychosomatic illness Possible destructive and ruthless behavior Can be very demanding, and even cruel to partner when Pluto is in the 7th House Problems with relation ships that can lead to divorce Antisocial personality Public relations ability in Opposition |

## Pluto with the Midheaven:

| Conjunction | Sextile, Trine | Square, Opposition |
| --- | --- | --- |
| Tremendous power in career The Aspects of a leader who wields influence over the masses | Strong desire for successful career The power and strength for career prominence Organizing ability | Anti-social tendencies Problems and delays in in career Tremendous desire for power |

Probable fame
This powerful influence
can be used for good
or evil

Natural authority
The ability to stay at
the top
Intuitive ability in career
Career can be in science,
the occult or spiritual
fields

The Sextile brings many
opportunities to advance
career

The Trine brings ease in
achieving career goals
with few obstacles
Career is often benefitted
through family
Constructive understanding
and use of power

Possible public disgrace or
notoriety
The Opposition often pro-
duces reckless daring
Possible overactive sex
drive
There can be problems
involving the family and/
or authority figures

## AFTERWORD

When I tell people about astrology, I feel like the World War II intelligence officers who broke the Japanese Naval code. I'm so excited about the breakthrough that I want to translate everything! But I have forced myself in this book to stick to the basics. From the basics, astrology is layered learning getting richer and richer from self-understanding and understanding of what makes other people tick. Astrology has made me more accepting of the differences in people than any other thing in my life. In learning, astrology is like the mother-lode in the gold mine of life.

In a sense, the key of understanding through astrology makes me think of the Rosetta Stone. The ability to read ancient Egyptian hieroglyphics was lost for many centuries. A French scholar deciphered the stone in 1822 unlocking the riches of the Egyptian antiquities. Astrology unlocks the richness of self-understanding.

There have been three times in my life when my mind has been blown open in an exciting dynamic way. The first time happened when I was in grade school and studied geography. I was fascinated to learn that an interesting, different world existed way beyond my neighborhood and city. The second mind-expanding event occurred when I was in college, and took a course in Logic. I still remember talking with my mother just after the first class. I told her that I never dreamed that people thought about such marvelous, abstract ideas. The third time happened when I began studying astrology. It is a mind-boggling field of study. I saw proof for the existence of God through the order of the universe!

There are many wonderful areas of study ahead — Transits and Progressions, Chart comparisons, in-depth study of each Planet in each Sign, further study of the Aspects, and learning how to integrate and interpret a Chart fully, and many more specialized areas of astrology.

My students have heard me say that I feel as if I'm doing a scene from "Lifestyles of the Rich and Famous" when I'm preparing for a class. I imagine that I have this huge closet — as big as a house — filled with beautiful things. It's hard to know which "gorgeous outfits" to select to study in each class. I hope astrology will make you feel the same way!

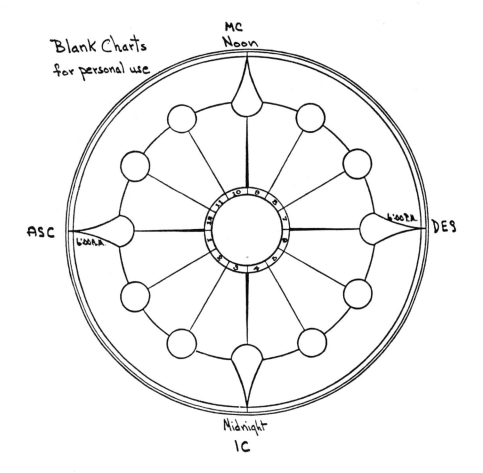

MC
Noon

Blank Charts
for personal use

ASC

DES

Midnight
IC

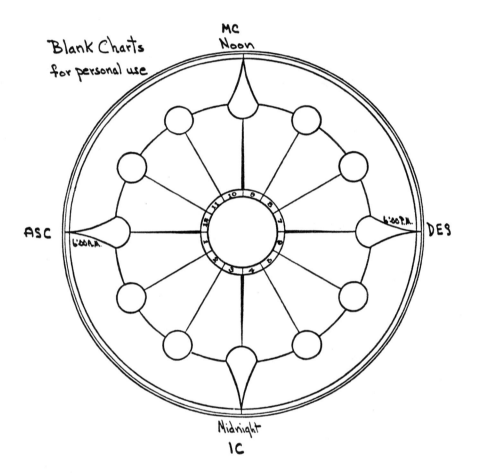

Blank Charts
for personal use